THE MAKING OF A JEW

THE MAKING OF A JEW

EDGAR M. BRONFMAN

G. P. PUTNAM'S SONS
NEW YORK

G. P. Putnam's Sons
Publishers Since 1838
200 Madison Avenue
New York, NY 10016

Library of Congress Cataloging-in-Publication Data
Bronfman, Edgar M., date.
The making of a Jew / by Edgar M. Bronfman.
p.   cm.
ISBN 0-399-14220-7
1. Bronfman, Edgar M., date.   2. Jews — Québec (Province) —
Montréal — Biography.   3. World Jewish Congress.   4. Jews — Politics
and government — 1948 –.   5. Montréal (Québec) — Biography.   I. Title.
F1054.5.M89J534   1996
971.4′2803′092 — dc20   [B]   96-17787   CIP

Printed in the United States of America
1   3   5   7   9   10   8   6   4   2

This book is printed on acid-free paper. ∞

Book design by Debbie Glasserman

*To the memory of all my grandparents, who yearned
to be free and braved the harsh realities of western
Canada to bring up their children in the New World,
and to the memory of my parents, whose lives
were an inspiration.*

CONTENTS

On Sunday morning, December 10, 1995, I stood with a *kipa* on my head on a platform at Madison Square Garden. I was there as President of the World Jewish Congress, and the event was a rally in memory of the slain Prime Minister, Yitzhak Rabin, and in support of Jewish unity and the Israeli government's struggle for peace in the Middle East.

The idea for the rally came to me on the plane home from Rabin's funeral in Israel the month before. I thought it important that something be done to galvanize the American Jewish community into supporting the government of Shimon Peres, to pay proper tribute to Rabin and to permit the Chief Rabbi of Israel to affirm that in our religion life is the most sacred thing of all. God gave it, and only God can take it away.

I discussed the idea with my fellow passengers Israel Singer and Elan Steinberg, respectively Secretary General and Executive Director of the World Jewish Congress, and we tried to analyze the risks. Extreme right-wing groups would almost certainly mount protests, and then television news reporters might portray ours as a fragmented community. An equally large risk would be if we couldn't fill the hall, which would be worse than no rally. On the other hand, if we succeeded, the rewards would be great: not only would the community unite, but those who were still fighting the peace process would be isolated, and perhaps could be induced to soften their rhetoric and increase their tolerance for other points of view.

We got to work as soon as we landed, the organizing groups meeting almost daily as they set about the task of insuring the presence of students, and locating Jewish groups that could be bused to the Garden. Israel Singer is well known and widely respected in the Orthodox community, and he worked hard to include as many of them as possible at the event. As for myself, I was still nervous—but then two things happened: the White House confirmed that Vice President Al Gore would attend and speak at the rally, and I spoke with Prime Minister Peres in Jerusalem.

You cannot let the "crazies" win by default, he argued to me. You must proceed. And so we did. The date was Friday morning, December 8, only two days before the scheduled day of the rally.

It was bitter cold but clear that Sunday as my wife, Jan, my brother, Charles, and his wife, Andy, and I made our way to Madison Square Garden. The security was unbelievably tight, and we watched as long lines approached the metal-detection machines. We were taken in through a special door and were led to our seats. I sat there, worriedly watching as people slowly filed in, aware of the reason for the delays, but silently praying for the house to fill. A huge picture of Yitzhak Rabin served as a backdrop. Just as I sighed in relief that it looked like the Garden would be full, Prime Minister Peres, Vice President Gore, Rabin's widow, Leah, and Chief Rabbi Lau, together with Governor Pataki of New York, many congressmen, and tons (it seemed) of security people marched in to their appointed seats, and the rally began. As agreed, I was the opening speaker, and I tried to set the tone:

"Vice President Gore, Prime Minister Peres, Mrs. Leah Rabin, Chief Rabbi Lau, *chaverim, chaverot,* friends. We are gathered here today to pay tribute to the memory of Prime

Minister Yitzhak Rabin, to offer our condolences to Leah Rabin, her children and her grandchildren, to demonstrate the unity of the Jewish people in support of the government of Prime Minister Shimon Peres, and to pray for peace in the Middle East. Just as we are gathered here, affiliates of the World Jewish Congress are holding similar rallies in Great Britain, Italy, Argentina, and France, to name a few.

"Yitzhak Rabin was my friend. I loved him as well as admired him for his strength, his bravery, his love of Israel and the Jewish people, his wisdom, and his total honesty. I remember well the reluctance he showed at that famous handshake scene on the White House lawn, and how that handshake started a whole new era in Israeli-Arab relations. At his funeral, I recall the words of King Hussein of Jordan, calling Yitzhak his brother and Leah his sister—an acknowledgment of more than peace—of friendship, even of love. And I remember the representation of heads of state and of government at that unbelievably sorrowful event, paying homage to his memory and by attribution to the Jewish State and the Jewish people.

"I recall with pride the words of our President, Bill Clinton, on that same occasion. He, too, prayed for peace and uttered the Hebrew words *'Hoo yuh-usseh shalom, aleinu v-ul col Yisrael, v-yimeru amen.'* I call on everyone here, and in the

United States of America and throughout the world, to carry a commitment to Yitzhak Rabin's vision of peace. Whatever our differences, let us vow to discuss them with civility and mutual respect.

"Life must go on. Shimon Peres did not expect to be Prime Minister again, but the cowardly work of a filthy assassin has bestowed that enormous responsibility on him. Already he has bound many wounds, brought unity to the people of Israel, and he will now bring them peace. For this we all pray. Shimon is a friend to me and to every Jew in the world. He is a savant, a man of dreams who understands the realities; a man of vision, courage, and strength; Yitzhak Rabin's partner in peace, and a partner in the building of the economies of his neighbors so that peace will bring a better life to all the inhabitants of the region.

"I wish to express my heartfelt gratitude to the other conveners of this great gathering, who helped make this moment possible—a moment in which we look back in sorrow and forward with hope."

Then I turned toward the huge picture of the slain Prime Minister, and in the words of President Clinton, said, *"Shalom, chaver."*

As I finished my speech, the lights dimmed, and a film on Rabin's life began. I stood there, gazing out into the dark, as thousands of faces gazed back, and I suddenly felt outside myself, looking back over a lifetime. What was I doing here, in this place? As a young man growing up, Judaism had meant little to me; in fact, much of my life had given secularity new meaning. Yet here I was, at the age of sixty-six, a Jewish leader and, more than that, a committed Jew.

As I made my way to my seat and the film of Rabin's illustrious life unrolled on the giant screen, I began to look back upon my own life, at over six decades of slow evolution—at the making of a Jew.

CHAPTER 1

MR. SAM

I was born in Montreal, in the province of Quebec, Canada, on June 20, 1929, the third child of Samuel and Saidye Bronfman, but, mark you well, the first son. I was preceded by Minda and then Phyllis, and followed two years later by Charles. Montreal was then Canada's largest, and by far its worldliest, city. The population, about one and a quarter million souls, was divided into linguistic and religious groupings; all the French speakers, by far the largest group, were Catholic; they were followed by the English Protestants, then by the English-speaking Catholics, mostly of Irish origin, and then by some 65,000 English-speaking Jews.

By most standards of the day, my father was a rich man,

and shortly after my birth the family moved to 15 Belvedere Road, in Westmount, the suburb of Montreal where the rich lived, and where my mother dwelt, until last July, when she died at the age of ninety-eight and a half. I had a confusing and a mostly unhappy childhood there. There were many live-in servants: a butler, a parlor maid, an upstairs maid, a cook, a kitchen maid, a nurse for my brother and me, and a mademoiselle for my sisters. There was also a laundress who came by day, as did the gardener, and the chauffeur, who lived with his wife and daughter in an apartment over the garage.

My parents had an unusual and loving relationship, unusual because my father spent so much time away from home when we were growing up. He was building an empire, and in the spirits business, the major market was the United States of America. He spent almost every week there, coming home on Saturday mornings and leaving again on Sunday nights, commuting, as it were, by train.

My mother's family, the Rosners, had been farmers in Plum Coulee, Manitoba, before they'd moved to Winnipeg, where Sam met Saidye. It was an hour's drive from the provincial capital. In fact, Gramps, as we affectionately called him, had been the mayor, chief of police, and captain of the fire department in Plum Coulee, because he also owned the general store. He leased the farms to others to operate. Gramma

Rosner was a sour-faced woman, as I remember — in fact, the only time I ever heard her laugh was when I pulled a prank. Gramps had told us that the way a Jewish man indicated his desire to have sex with his wife was by putting his yarmulke on her bedpost. During a seder one evening, I asked to be excused to go to the bathroom, rushed upstairs, and put a yarmulke on Gramma's bedpost. Later that evening, as they retired, we heard chortles and guffaws coming from the guest room.

Father had convinced the world that he was six years older than Mother, and that he had been born in Brandon, Manitoba, in 1891. After his death on July 10, 1971, I went through his papers and found an old passport that indicated he had been born in Bessarabia in 1889. Clearly, his motivation had not been to try to make himself younger, but to establish that he had been born in Canada rather than Russia. The Soviet Union was lustily hated, and if he were to get the honors he so keenly desired, he obviously thought it better to seem to be Canadian-born. Of course, we also grew up with the story that upon his birth, his father had declared that he was not going to give three sons to the Czar for gunpowder, and decided to go to Canada. This did not jibe with my father's claim of having been born in Canada, but nobody seemed to notice, or perhaps we were all so overwhelmed by his awesome and frightening presence that no one dared ask.

Ekiel and Minnie Bronfman had brought four children from somewhere near Kishinev, Bessarabia—what we now call Moldova—to a small town in Saskatchewan in about 1891. Ekiel had brought with him a sack of tobacco seeds—evidently that is what he had done for a living back home—and a *melamed*, a teacher for his young family. It is symptomatic of that era that people had no idea of the geography of this new land they were adopting. The climate of Saskatchewan was much too harsh to grow tobacco, and Ekiel left his Minnie, Abe, Harry, Laura, and Sam behind while he went to Brandon, Manitoba, to get established so that he could bring them all together there. My siblings and I know next to nothing about the early years of the Bronfman clan. That they were poor—very poor—is something we have learned, but all of Father's siblings—including four more children, Jean, Bee, Allan, and Rose, born in Brandon—always conducted a conspiracy of silence. Perhaps it was out of respect for their parents—Ekiel had not set the world on fire.

I never knew either Minnie or Ekiel. She died in the flu epidemic that followed the First World War, and he died of stomach cancer some four or five years thereafter. The first-born, Abe, was no businessman. He liked to play cards, was probably a womanizer in his youth, and never worked very hard. Harry, the next brother, was a worker. We have his account of how he used to sell frozen fish during the winter. He'd take them great distances in a horse-drawn vehicle—and he wrote that he was proud that the family always waited Friday-night dinner until he returned. Laura, the only sister older than Sam, was penurious to a fault. One of her sisters once told her in my presence, "They don't put pockets on shrouds."

And then came Sam.

Let me describe my father. He wasn't tall, barely five feet five, with sandy-colored hair, which was thinning as I first remember it, piercing blue eyes, and a prominent but straight nose. He had a round face, and Mother used to refer to it, in the words of the famous Eddie Cantor song, as her "baby face." He had a well-developed stomach, as would befit a gentleman of that age—a certain girth was a sign of prosperity. When we were all together, Phyllis would sometimes call the paunch "Mary," as if he were pregnant, but he had to be in a good mood for her to try that sort of frivolity. He dressed conservatively and always looked neat, although he was too short and rotund to be called elegant.

I don't know where it came from, but Samuel Bronfman was driven. His father had not been particularly successful, and his poor mother (that's how he always described her) had a problem keeping eight children in decent clothing. Father grew up to detest poverty. He couldn't stand the hand-me-down, patched clothing of his youth, and as a result, Charles and I were forced at one time to wear Eton collars and jackets.

From the time he was a youngster, Sam was determined to be someone. I should have capitalized those words, for they were the driving force in his life. He was very insecure, and I guess I was always troubled by the fact that by the time he did get to be someone, he hardly believed it.

The combination of his insecurity and his insatiable need for recognition probably accounted for his fabled temper. He had the bad habit of using language "that would make a sailor blush." He seemed to be not only impatient, but genuinely put upon by everything that didn't go exactly as he had wanted. I know that I always felt that someday that temper could be turned on me, and I built up defenses against that happening. The most important of these was my rejection not only of him, but of his Judaism. I did it most consciously in my late teens and early twenties, so that by the time I was married and having children, I had rejected not just Judaism, but religion in general, at least on an emotional level.

There were two sides to Samuel Bronfman's life. "Being someone" meant being both a successful businessman and a community leader. Part of his insecurity had its roots in Prohibition. His career started in the hotel business in western Canada. He had first been assigned there, whether by his father or his brother Harry or a combination of both isn't clear, to help his big brother Abe, whose hotel wasn't doing very well, probably because Abe was lazy and gambled too much. When he was old enough, Sam bought the Bell Hotel in Winnipeg, which was the acorn seed of the tall oak he would later grow. Canada's Prohibition was different from the one in the United States, because its constituent provinces had much more power, comparatively speaking, than did the American states. Each province prohibited shipping wines and spirits within its own boundaries, but for a while it stayed legal to ship them between provinces, so that's what the Bronfmans did. Eventually, all the provinces took over the wholesaling and most of the retailing themselves. The last to do so was Quebec, and perhaps that's why the family moved to Montreal in 1922. Finally, with all the selling in the hands of the provinces, if one wanted to stay in the beverage-alcohol business, one had to become a distiller.

Father and his brothers built a distillery in a town called

Ville LaSalle, just outside Montreal near the St. Lawrence River, in 1924. He and his brother Allan had flown to England to meet with Thomas Hurd, the managing director of the British combine called the Distillers Corporation Ltd., and, against all odds, convinced him to invest in this fledgling enterprise. The products were called Highland Whiskies, and they consisted of a blend of grain whiskies made on a Coffee still (named for its inventor) and malt whiskies produced in Scotland by the DCL. How many of these products were sold in Canada, and how many were shipped to bootleggers, who in turn sold them in the United States, I don't know. But from the beginning of their experience in the beverage-alcohol business until the end of American Prohibition, the Bronfmans dealt with bootleggers. Father always maintained that they never did anything illegal, and that, I am sure, was technically true. But they had storage facilities on the French-owned islands of St. Pierre and Miquelon in the Gulf of St. Lawrence, where goods were kept ready to be transshipped across the American border.

Then, in 1928, the Seagram family of Waterloo, Ontario, found they had to make a choice. Short of funds, they had to sell either their string of racehorses or their distillery—they couldn't fund both. Luckily for us, they decided to sell the tiny distillery, and the Bronfmans bought it. The company they had established was called Distillers Corporation Ltd.—they were partners with the British combine—and so in 1928, the Bronfmans and DCL formed a holding company called Distillers Corporation–Seagrams Ltd., which owned the Quebec and Ontario operations. After Father's death, that holding company's name was changed to The Seagram Company Ltd., the name it bears today. I did that to make it easier for investors to find the listing in the newspapers.

When it became legal to sell beverage alcohol in the United States, Father decided to enter the U.S. market as a manufacturer. The DCL in Britain preferred to ship their whiskies to agents in every market, and that included the United States, and so there was a parting of the ways. Fortunately, Father had talked the DCL into giving the Bronfmans the right to buy them out should there be a major disagreement. He once told me the story of how he had convinced them. Evidently, he had quoted Tennyson: "To a man, love is but a part, to a woman, her whole existence." To the DCL, the Canadian enterprise was a part, he'd continued, but to him, it was his whole existence. They'd agreed.

Shortly after buying out his partner, and thus going deeply into debt, Sam Bronfman got a strep throat and, I gather, came close to death. As he once told me, I might have been not only an orphan, but a destitute one at that. The orphan part I really didn't mind, I tell Seagram groups as I recount the firm's history. It's a quip—with unfortunately more truth than poetry to it.

After Prohibition ended, the United States government took the Canadian distillers to court, to try to levy taxes on goods brought illegally into the country. There was much publicity, and for a man who so desperately wanted to be someone, this notoriety, this association with the underworld, was devastating. It was a great big stone Father carried with him his whole life. The shame he had felt as a youngster growing up in poverty came back with full force, and it never stopped hurting. His constant lashing out, his tantrums, were most probably a result of those frustrations.

Anti-Semitism was palpable in Montreal. There were restricted hotels (no dogs or Jews allowed), and Jews were not welcome on the boards of the banks or of McGill University, Montreal's fabled institute of learning. The powers-that-were had little, if any, social contact with Jews, and very little business dealings, except occasionally on a professional level, and what little contact there was occurred because of charitable endeavors. In the mid-thirties, the Bronfmans were established as a leading Jewish family—if not *the* leading Jewish family—precisely because of their ability to give large amounts of money to charity. Father soon became the head of many charity drives. When World War II began, Father was as supportive of the war effort as one could possibly be, and became the leading Jew on the national scene as well, and finally President of the Canadian Jewish Congress, a position he would hold for eighteen years. That support was based on his love of everything that England and the British Empire stood for: the liberal tradition that had allowed families like ours to do so well—and the fact that Hitler was systematically destroying European Jewry.

Indeed, Father became more English than those who lived in Britain. He believed that Canada, the inheritor of English libertarianism, had made it possible for Jews to live as *almost* first-class citizens under the Union Jack. Early on he knew, and thus we knew, that the Nazis were murdering Jews, and I remember being scared. What would happen if we were to lose the war? Would we all be killed? How well I recall Pearl Harbor Day, "a date which will live in infamy," and how glad I was that the great United States was in the war, for that meant that the Allies would win, and that Hitler would not exterminate us.

Thus it was easy to understand that the Jewish community was very supportive of the war. Neither Father nor any of his friends would ever have dreamed of doing anything that would make that community look anything less than superpatriotic.

Mother took on the responsibility of organizing the Jewish women of Montreal for the war effort, and was at her station daily, from morning until early evening. The organization of which she was president, the Jewish branch of the Canadian Red Cross, employed over 7,000 women volunteers, who made bandages and knitted sweaters and socks for Canada's servicemen. For that work, in 1943, Mother was awarded the O.B.E., the Order of the British Empire. Now, a glance at the *Who's Who* of Canada during the war and shortly thereafter would also reveal Father's many duties in the war effort, including a post in the highest civilian group, the War Production Board—but when Father heard the news at his office, he called Mother, who was sixty miles away, at our other house in Ste. Marguerite, and insisted she come to Montreal immediately. When she arrived, he made a courtly bow, and said, "The King thinks as highly of you as I do."

I think this was his best moment ever. Clearly, he was also entitled to the honor, but because of the Bronfman family's activities during Prohibition, and the residue of bad feelings in the West toward his brother Harry, the powers-that-be had decided to avoid political damage by giving the honor to Mother. And Father played it straight.

But still, it must have rankled. His closest collaborator—Father never really had friends—was the family lawyer, Lazarus Phillips. Between them they had an interesting arrangement in the battle for who would be "the first Jew in Canada to . . ." The year was 1952. The deal was that Laz would run for Parliament, from what was thought to be a safe district, with all the support the Bronfman family could give him. He would then become a member of the Cabinet, thus becoming the first Jew to get whatever ministry they had in mind, and from there use his influence to have Sam Bronfman appointed to the Senate. This wish to become a Canadian senator became an obsession, and when Laz lost his election to a Socialist who showed pictures of the large Phillips house in Westmount to the mostly working-class constituents, the game seemed to be over. But Laz had an ego, too, and he decided that *he* would get appointed to the Senate, although it was now too late to be the first Jew to do so. That made attorney Phillips a mortal enemy of Sam Bronfman, and the language Father used to describe a man whom he had often called his best friend was beyond foul, another lesson for me that this man could turn on anyone—meaning me. Consciously or subconsciously, I lived with this all my life, and the idea that I was only conditionally loved was reinforced by what I observed of Father's conduct toward others.

Actually, the battle with Laz was neither the first nor the last of its kind. Father seemed to be in need of someone to feud with—to swear at. It seemed almost a physical as well as a psychological necessity. He started feuding with his brother Allan in the mid-fifties, and that never ended until Father's death. The reason for that feud, outwardly, was that Allan kept saying "we," and supposedly taking credit for the great success that Father felt he had achieved despite his family, rather than with it. Deeper, though, there was a certain jealousy. Sam had put Allan through law school, and Allan actually had been a lawyer with Sam's firm of attorneys, Andrews and Andrews, in Winnipeg. Allan was well spoken, and Sam felt undereducated. Worst of all, Allan told his wife and children that he was an equal partner, and that galled Sam to no end.

I remember a trip we took with Uncle Allan one summer when I was seventeen. Charles was fifteen, Allan's older son, Edward, was eighteen, and Peter, the younger son, was less than four months younger than I. Uncle Allan had rented a yacht on Georgian Bay, where the fishing was supposed to be very good. It was an unfortunate excursion. Aunt Lucy, Allan's wife, was along, as was some young college student who Allan had thought might be useful. The fishing was lousy, the bugs were more than plentiful, the weather was sultry, and everyone was somewhat depressed and off their feed. An incident occurred, in which Charles was a wise guy, and Uncle Allan gave him hell. Then Charles compounded matters by telling Uncle Allan not to yell at him or he would tell "the boss," referring, of course, to Father. Allan really blew his cool, and I interrupted quietly, suggesting that Allan take us to the nearest port, where he would kindly arrange for a Seagram person to drive us home to Montreal. Allan knew that I was fully aware of the financial situation between the two families: all the Seagram shares owned by trusts that had been created for the benefit of Allan's and Sam's children and grandchildren were all in one holding company, Seco Investments, Ltd. This company in turn was owned (67.8 percent) by CEMP Investments, Ltd., which stood for Charles, Edgar, Minda, and Phyllis, and the remaining 32.2 percent was owned by Edper Investments, Ltd., which stood for Edward and Peter. We controlled Seagram and had a lot more financial firepower than he did.

Allan must have been worried that I'd tell Father how he

had browbeaten Charles, and bribed us all with a cancellation of the yacht trip and a return to Gananoque in the Thousand Islands, where we had spent happy times in years gone by. This story is told to illustrate the effect Father had on people. He scared them. Me, too.

CHAPTER 2

A THORN AMONG ROSES

The educational system in Montreal was based on language. Thus, all the Protestants, the English-speaking Catholics, and the Jews went to the same schools, either public or private. My sister Minda was sent to a public school for the first part of her life, but she and then Phyllis were educated at a private school called The Study. I was sent to Selwyn House School at the age of six, which was normal, as kindergarten and preschool were hardly known in Montreal.

Selwyn House was the school for the Protestant elite of Montreal, and competed with another English-speaking private school, Lower Canada College. (Canada originally had been split between Upper Canada, now Ontario, and Lower

Canada, now Quebec.) There were few Jewish boys, just the Goldblooms, sons of Montreal's most famous pediatrician, and the Ballons, sons of the most famous ear, nose, and throat specialist. The school was owned by Geoffrey Wanstall, a martinet Englishman who ran the school as if it were an English public school, and handed out corporal punishment as he deemed proper. Classes went as far as the sophomore year in high school; one had to complete the last two years of high school elsewhere, and most boys went to boarding school. It was definitely Protestant-oriented, with the Lord's Prayer recited daily, but that was the only religious activity. I didn't mind that prayer, because it had no mention of Jesus. However, when my mother asked me how my first day of school had gone, I remember saying that I didn't like being called Bronfman. They could, I declared, call me either Edgar or Mr. Bronfman, but not just Bronfman.

My brother Charles was quite sick when he was two years old, and a trained nurse was hired to help him recuperate. Her name was Helen MacDonald; she was quite diminutive, and we called her Cutie. Don't let the nickname confuse you, though, as she was quite the disciplinarian. She stayed with us another nine years. It was she who basically brought us up, since my father was busy commuting to New York, and during the war, my mother went to work as President of the Jewish Women's Red Cross in Montreal. Cutie did a good job, but I hated having someone between me and my parents, especially between me and my mother. And so when I was bar mitzvahed and Cutie asked me what I would like as a present, my answer was, "Your resignation." To her credit, she wasn't offended, and she did leave, but my mother didn't get it at all. She simply hired another woman to take care of Charles and me. The woman was a younger blonde, and quite attractive, but I didn't want anyone between my mother and me any longer!

Almost from the start, I was confused as to my identity. We led a Jewish life, in the Conservative tradition, at home; I went to Sunday school and junior congregation at the Sha'ar Hashomayin (Gates of Heaven) synagogue in Westmount. I had, almost from the start, two sets of friends: those at Selwyn House, and those at the synagogue. My impression is that my daily life was more important to father, probably because he asked about my grades at school, and never mentioned anything that had to do with my religious education, if one wanted to call it that. Perhaps for that reason, I paid little attention to what went on in Sunday school, skipped classes as I grew older, and hardly ever went to junior congregation.

In my schoolwork I was not what I would call a great student, but I was always facile—it came easily, and I didn't have to work very hard to get decent grades. At Selwyn House we were graded every week as either first or second and so on. I determined to come second, because if I did any better I would always be expected to come first, and that was something I didn't want to cope with.

Charles and I took other lessons, as well: Hebrew lessons from a Lithuanian refugee named Luba Gordon, horseback riding, as well as the piano. Note that my sisters did not have to take Hebrew lessons—Judaism is a male-chauvinist religion. As for the rest, my parents must have thought that young, well-bred English boys took horseback-riding and piano lessons. Remember that my father was a great Anglophile, and worshiped everything British. The worst lessons we had to take were Father's "lessons in life." At Sunday lunch, we were all treated to endless monologues, as if delivered from Mount Sinai—moralistic sermons. But sex was absolutely never discussed. Perhaps if there had been some sex education along with the homilies, it wouldn't have been so tedious. In any case, I perceived that the non-Jewish side of my education was considered more important than the religious, and that's the way I conducted myself.

Richard Joel, the charming and charismatic head of International Hillel, an organization that provides services to Jews on campuses throughout North America, and now in Russia and Hungary as well as Ukraine, tells a remarkably poignant story. It's about a priest, a minister, and a rabbi. The priest was complaining about the mice that had infested the cathedral.

"One day," he said, "I hired a flautist, at great expense, and he piped the mice some five miles out of town. I thought I was rid of them, but in five days they were back."

The minister said, "Extraordinary that you should have the same problem I have. My church is also infested with mice, and one Monday we trapped them all and took them twenty miles away in the countryside and scattered them. Ten days later, they had returned."

Then the rabbi said, "My synagogue was also infested with mice. But I had a different experience. I gathered them all around me, then I held up my arms and told them, 'Congratulations, you are all bar mitzvahs.' I haven't seen or heard of any of them since."

I, too, was bar mitzvahed. It was a heavenly day, and since I had been born on my parents' seventh anniversary, I was bar mitzvahed on their twentieth. And the twentieth fell on a Saturday in 1942, a perfect coincidence. It was a perfect June day. I did my reading in the synagogue, and as I stood beneath the raised platform, the rabbi held forth with his right arm outstretched and pronounced the traditional blessing on me. I felt in great awe. Recently I was asked at a meeting of Hillel members at the University of Miami what the most meaningful spiritual moment of my life was. I immediately said that it was this benediction, closely followed by the time when, knowing I would never see him again, I asked my grandfather to do the same benediction, which he did as my eyes flowed with tears.

At 15 Belvedere Road, there was a luncheon in my honor, and a fruitcake, baked for me by my cousin Allan Bronfman, Jr., which weighed forty pounds. It was followed that evening by a dinner dance honoring my parents' twentieth anniversary, and we were allowed to stay up late and enjoy the music, the night, and the great bonhomie that filled the air. For about two weeks thereafter, I put on tefillin, and then, just like the rabbi's mice in the story, I left Judaism behind.

From Selwyn House, I was sent—I had absolutely no choice about the decision—to Trinity College School in Port Hope, Ontario. I don't know whether or not my parents knew it, but I was the first Jew ever to attend that school. In Montreal there might have been fierce "first Jew" competition among my father and his colleagues, but I assure you I did not compete for this so-called honor. Just to give you an idea, until my headmaster, Philip Ketchum, every head had been a bishop of the Anglican Church.

The anti-Semitism was there. It wasn't so much of the in-your-face variety as it was remarks that one could hear around corners. I had a major argument with Mr. Ketchum about church attendance. I argued that it was not right to compel me to go to church every day and twice on Sundays, and we finally agreed that I needed to go only once on Sunday. Seen with the clarity of 20-20 hindsight, it was a stupid argument. As it wasn't the school's fault that I was there, I should have had to go simply as a matter of discipline, or I shouldn't have had to go at all. I really hated that school, but nowhere near as much as my brother did when it became his time. Trinity had the typical English new-boy system, by which, whatever your age, you were made to suffer stupid indignities, along with boys one, two, and sometimes three years younger. A new boy had to have all the buttons of his jacket buttoned, which quickly ruined the jacket. He had to shine his own shoes and those of some seniors, and hold the door open for seniors and, of course, masters. Every new boy got whipped by the prefects with a bat that new boys were required to fashion in the woodworking shop. I deeply resented this treatment and thought it unfair and stupid, and so I got beaten for no other reason except my attitude. Bloody damn right!

There were some light moments. In my second and final year, I became very good at billiards. My father had started out in the hotel business, remember, which in western Canada was a euphemism for a bar with a few shabby rooms upstairs, and a pool table. If the owners/managers weren't good at pool, they could easily lose the profits at the table. My father didn't lose any profits, and as we grew up he would give us occasional lessons at our pool table at 15 Belvedere Road. I had a match with one of the masters one evening, the same night as the Easter pageant. This bit of entertainment had not been made compulsory, and word got around that Mr. Gwynn-Timothy and I were going to have an English billiards match. There were as many boys in there as the small room would allow, and the master was reprimanded for not having set a better example by attending the pageant. To make matters worse for him, I won.

There's one more story from this time in my life that I'd like to relate. During the summer when I was fourteen, I got a job as a caddy on the nine-hole golf course at an inn about a mile and a half from a lovely estate my parents had rented in Ste. Marguerite Station in the Laurentian Mountains. The inn was a restricted hotel, which I didn't know, but the golf pro needed an English-speaking caddy, and asked me if I would work for a Mr. Kenney, who came from New York and played fourteen holes every day. I negotiated with him and got the job. Under the terms of our agreement, I was also allowed to play golf in the afternoons myself.

One day I brought my cousin Irving and his father, Peter Groper, who had married my father's sister Jean, to play golf. After we were through, the golf pro came to me and asked me not to bring Uncle Peter and Irving back. They looked too Jewish. It was the first time I had ever encountered this kind of anti-Semitism, and I was deeply, deeply hurt, and uncomprehending. I thought that's what we were fighting a war about. I told my parents about the incident, but I never did get the kind of explanation I wanted. It's stuck with me all these years, and to this day fuels some of my drive against anti-Semitism.

———

After I graduated from Trinity, I went to Williams College in Williamstown, Massachusetts. It's hard to believe, but I had no real choice about that, either. My parents didn't ever discuss with me which college I wanted, or what course, or where I wanted to continue my studies geographically, indeed even if I wanted to continue my studies. All I know is that I went once, was interviewed by the dean of admissions,

Frederick Copeland, was accepted, and in the fall of 1946, I found myself enrolled as a student.

I must have been very naïve and unaware of my surroundings. I was such a young seventeen-year-old, so used to the discipline of Belvedere Road, Selwyn House, and Trinity, and here I was in very strange surroundings. One of the first things that freshmen experienced in their first few weeks at Williams was being rushed for admission into a fraternity. How was I supposed to know that at the time Williams had a 5 percent limit on Jews overall, and that by national charter and probably by local preference very few of the fraternities accepted *any* Jews? There seemed to be a pattern here—first a prep school where I was the first Jew ever, and then an American college that clearly was not overfriendly to members of my tribe. To this day, I do not know what my parents were trying to accomplish with this bizarre treatment. I can figure out that Father was trying to train an heir to an empire, but his background—the bringing of a *melamed* from Russia, his insistence on synagogue attendance on the Jewish holidays, which in and of itself made my brother and me different from our classmates, and we all know how young kids like that—seemed to be in total contradiction with his actions.

In a way, I can understand that he wanted his children to

be free from the restraints that being Jewish had meant to him, his wife, and his siblings. Perhaps he reasoned that our generation would be rich enough and important enough that we would successfully break down those barriers. But did he have to make it that hard for us to be Jewish? Underneath, he must have had some deeply held antipathy toward his religion and his religious experience to have made him act the way he did. I don't believe he was ignorant of what his actions might lead to. I don't much believe in coincidences, either.

For reasons that escaped me then, and still do, I was assigned to a course called "Corrective Composition," supposedly because I couldn't express myself using the English language. I wrote an essay on the evils of the fraternity system, and handed it over to an assistant professor in the English department. He said that he didn't understand why I had been assigned to Corrective Comp, released me, and added that he was sorry I hadn't made it into a fraternity house. I replied that I had, in fact—but that the system was still evil. There was even a place called Garfield House, where those who hadn't made it into a fraternity, or who didn't want to join, all ended up—you had to be in a fraternity or the Garfield House if you just wanted to eat.

In North Adams, about five miles east of Williamstown,

there was a shul, and my freshman year was the only time I attended Yom Kippur services. That experience had no meaning for me, however, and I abandoned all thoughts of continuing regular holiday shul participation. Come to think of it, I don't remember whether other Jewish undergraduates attended that shul in any number, either.

Williams College was not co-educational then, but Bennington College, a women's institution of higher learning, was some seventeen miles north of Williamstown, just across the Vermont border. One of the great problems in Jewish life today is that assimilation is so acceptable to the Gentiles, and thus very easy, especially on the campus. Boy meets girl, they fall in love, very often they marry, and if one of them is a Jew, then that one is usually lost to the Jewish people. When I went to college, I soon began dating, and I didn't care whether or not the girl was Jewish. The result was that in the fall of my junior year, I managed to get engaged to an Irish beauty whom I had met the summer before. The engagement wasn't all that serious—I was just trying to get my parents' attention, and I think I did that.

The engagement was part of a general pattern of immaturity for me. I got into a lot of trouble at Williams, and after a couple of motor vehicle accidents, the last time on a motorcycle after a particularly "wet" party, I was allowed to resign.

I returned to Montreal, enrolled at McGill University, and tried to pull my act together. I was obviously furious with my father, and I sought the help of a practitioner of psycho-somatic medicine, named Ben Raginsky, to help me come to terms with myself. At McGill, I did reasonably well and graduated with honors, and although I went to synagogue on the important Jewish holidays, religion played absolutely no role in my life.

It was while I attended McGill that I met Ann Loeb, who by some coincidence had started at Bennington after I had left Williams. I met her by accident—she had called the St. Regis Hotel apartment that Father used as his New York City pied-à-terre because she needed a date for some fancy party—actually she needed a second date! Charles had met Ann the previous summer. Coincidentally, my mother was there, answered the phone, and told Ann that Charles was in Montreal and wouldn't be in New York for Thanksgiving, but that Edgar probably would be (I had loved going to New York from Williamstown, and I kept up the habit at McGill). We met, and the pursuit of Ann Loeb was begun. She was Jew-ish, and from a noble Jewish-American family that, through her mother, was related to the Lehmans, the Lewissohns, and the Altschuls, the cream of German Jewry. On her father's side, she was a Daughter of the American Revolution—her father's mother, Adeline Moses, could trace her U.S. lineage to before the American Revolution. I thought that the parents would be very pleased. I was about twenty-one and a half when we first met. We had a long and, for me, tortuous romance, and finally got engaged to be married two years later.

Ann's mother, Frances, was nicknamed "Peter." Actually, she had given this name to herself, because her mother had been so disappointed that the baby wasn't a boy that she had totally ignored her and hadn't named her for some time. The play *Peter Pan* was popular a few years after her birth, and so she decided to name herself "Peter." It stuck, and until her death, her grandchildren called her Petie. Frances Lehman died on Friday, May 17, 1996. Ann's father, John, worked with his father, Carl M. Loeb, at their family brokerage and banking business, Carl M. Loeb, Rhoades, and Co. The Rhoades part came from another brokerage firm with whom they had merged.

John and Peter Loeb were assimilationists, and so the clan was somewhat critical of Ann for marrying this Russian Jew, but married we were, in her parents' apartment at 730 Park Avenue, on January 10, 1953. I was twenty-three and a half, and Ann had turned twenty on September 19. Some thirteen days after the nine months' gestation period, Samuel II was born. The naming tells its own story. I knew Father would not be able to resist having the firstborn grandchild named after him, and I kind of liked the idea of doing something contrary to Jewish tradition. You're not supposed to name anyone after a living person, but only after a close relative who has recently died. Fortunately, as far as the synagogue was concerned, I was able to name him in Hebrew after my mother's father, whose "outside" name had been Samuel, but whose Hebrew name had been Shalom, whereas my father's Hebrew name was Zindel. Sammy, as we called him for many years thereafter, was circumcised, but there was no formal *brit*, the religious ceremony performed eight days after the birth of a son. Ann and I went the way of the Loebs rather than that of my parents, and that is certainly not to be blamed on Ann. Clearly, had I insisted on a Jewish ceremony and a Jewish home, she would have agreed, within certain limits, but since all the time we had been dating I had never obeyed any dietary laws, it was inconceivable to both of us that I would suddenly insist on a kosher home.

We had five children together, all born in Lenox Hill Hospital in New York, although we lived in Montreal until the third, Holly, was born in August of 1956 (the ob/gyn was Mortimer Rodgers, brother of the brilliant songwriter Richard Rodgers). There was absolutely no religion in our home whatsoever—no Friday-night service to welcome the

Sabbath, no observance of Jewish holidays, no education for those five kids about their Jewish background. I was not ashamed of being Jewish. The religion had nothing whatsoever to do with my behavior. I was simply still in rebellion against my father, and I actually went so far as to eat ham at our house in Westmount on Yom Kippur. (The fingers had a hard time writing that.) I worked at the Seagram plant at what was then called Ville LaSalle, as a blender, which is important to know only because Father seemed loath to come to the house for breakfast while he visited with his grandson. I soon figured out the reason—he was worried lest I eat bacon. I assured him that I could not, because my job as a blender demanded that my taste buds not be cluttered up with the smoky, lingering taste.

I stayed in Canada until after my twenty-sixth birthday, at which point I was no longer eligible for the United States draft. We moved to New York and settled in Purchase, where we rented a house while ours was being built on part of the land that Carl M. and Caroline Loeb had left after their demise. This was in December of 1955. I had belonged to the synagogue in Montreal, but I didn't bother looking for one in our new territory, either around Purchase or, later, after we moved to Manhattan, in New York City.

I was now an employee of Joseph E. Seagram & Sons, Inc.,

the holding company for all our American companies, which in turn was wholly owned by Distillers Corp.–Seagrams Ltd., the Canadian holding company that was listed on the New York, Montreal, and Toronto stock exchanges, and later would also be listed in London and Paris. My new job was as Chairman of the Administrative Committee, which meant I was in charge of everything but sales and marketing.

Being married to an American, I was able to apply for U.S. citizenship after three years of residence. I wanted to be an American because I liked politics, especially its discussion, and I have always felt that only citizens should be involved in such debate. In April of 1959, I went before a judge—in chambers—who started to ask me questions. I suggested that since I had spent two and a half years at an American institute of higher learning, it would be a terrible indictment on the country's educational system if I were not able to answer them, so why didn't he just ask me to raise my right hand and swear allegiance? He did just that. I am not sure that there was not a little rebelliousness in my decision, not only to be an American, but also to make sure that my children would also be born in the U.S. of A.

I was still "Mr. Sam" 's son and heir, however, and that meant a role not only in Seagram, but in his charities. Soon after I arrived in New York, Joe Willen, the Executive Director of the Federation of Jewish Philanthropies, asked to have lunch with me. We ate in the executive dining room, and during the course of the lunch, he asked me if I knew the difference between a Jew and a *goy*. Feigning ignorance, I listened as he proceeded to tell me the difference: When you ask a Jew to give to charity, the only question is how much; when you ask a *goy*, first of all you have to convince him that he *should* give. An exaggeration, but it's true: charity is part of the Jewish system of belief.

So I got involved in the New York Federation of Jewish Philanthropies and the UJA. I took over from Father the running of the special cocktail parties he held prior to each annual dinner, until the two organizations merged and there was only one big dinner. But this was fund-raising, and had nothing to do with religion.

Let me repeat. One of the problems that so many American Jews had at the time was that they expressed their Jewishness primarily through a check in support of Israel. I was the same. I was active for Israel, and for those in need in New York City, but in my heart and in my head it had nothing at all to do with the Jewish religion.

All that was about to change, through the intervention of one of the most remarkable figures in my life.

CHAPTER 3

NAHUM

Nahum Goldmann was an extraordinary figure, and had been a constant visitor to 15 Belvedere Road. He was about Father's height, with wavy silver hair and laughing blue eyes that could turn to ice, and was quite a ladies' man. Born in the Pale of Settlement, married to a wealthy German Jewish woman, and the father of two sons, Nahum was an early Zionist, and to me a wise man, at least when women were not concerned. When I first met him, Nahum was the President of the World Jewish Congress, which he had founded in 1936 with Rabbi Stephen Wise of New York to fight the battle for the survival of European Jewry against the oncoming Nazi onslaught. Father and Lord Israel

Sieff of England, the Chairman of Marks & Spencer, were the only two vice presidents. Like Nelson Rockefeller, Father never wanted to be vice president of anything, so I knew that Nahum had to be a very important man in his eyes. Together with their wives, Father and Nahum had traveled to San Francisco in 1946, when the United Nations Charter was being debated with a view to the creation of the State of Israel.

Father, too, was a Zionist, and had been very active in the securing of arms for the Israelis during Israel's War of Independence in 1948: I'd overheard conversations of his with various Canadian government officials persuading them to sell them arms. I was not at all involved in his work with the WJC, however. I was aware that a South African expatriate named Max Melamet spent quite some time in Father's New York office, but I was not invited in on those conversations, nor did I volunteer. I was consulted when Father decided to raise money from the beverage-alcohol industry, for the North American branch, of which he was Chairman, and I was aware of his disagreements with Prime Minister Golda Meir, who refused to be forthcoming when it came to peace overtures with the Arabs, but that was all.

He must have been very influenced in this latter view by Dr. Goldmann. As early as 1921, when discussing the Balfour Declaration, which was finally proclaimed in 1924, Nahum had said that in the long run, it didn't really matter what the British thought of a Jewish State in Palestine, it really only mattered what the Arabs thought. On the eve of Ben-Gurion's proclamation of the Jewish State, Goldmann had tried to get him to delay, saying that with a little time, he thought he would be able to convince the government of Egypt not to go to war. Then, after the Six-Day War, Nahum became an advocate of Yigal Allon, the Foreign Minister, who wanted to try to make peace with Israel's neighbors, as did Moshe Dayan, the Israeli hero and Minister of Defense. But Golda was a real hard-liner, who refused to acknowledge the existence of the Palestinian people, and even had Nahum deposed from his position as President of the World Zionist Organization, one he had long held, along with his other posts in Jewish life. That title is unconferred to this day. I heard all about this only after I got involved in the WJC, after Father's death in July 1971.

In the fall of that same year, Nahum approached me and asked if I would undertake to co-chair an international advisory body with Marcus Sieff, the son of Israel Sieff (who had died) and then the Chairman of Marks & Spencer. The idea was to meet three or four times a year, invite special guest speakers, and keep up with, or perhaps even lead, the Jewish world. We had three or four very good and interesting meetings, but there were two problems that I could not overcome.

One was that we were all so scattered throughout the world that it was extremely difficult to find a date convenient to even the majority of the members, and the other was that we ran out of pressing problems to engage the minds of these busy men. The advisory body was allowed to disappear quietly. Looking back, I am sure that this was simply Nahum's way of getting me deeply involved with the WJC, and perhaps even to succeed him. He was afraid I'd turn him down, though, until Max Melamet suggested that he ask me to become Chairman of the North American branch. According to Max, Nahum seemed surprised that Max thought I would accept, but I felt I owed it to Father's memory to try to do something with the WJC, and so I accepted.

The North American branch was made up of the Jewish communities in Canada, the United States, and, in those days, Mexico. Since then, Mexico has become part of the Latin American Jewish Congress. The other branches are the European, now known as the European Jewish Congress, the Israeli, the Southeast Asian, and that of the CIS, the former Soviet Union. The World Jewish Congress is an organization of organizations rather than of individuals, and yet we now have 150,000 paying members in the United States alone who definitely consider themselves part of the WJC family. The different constituent bodies have regular meetings, the Executive Committee meets twice a year and on an ad hoc

basis, whenever necessary, usually by telephone, the Governing Board, on which all the branches are represented, meets
every two years, and the Plenum, where all the countries
of the WJC gather for reports, initiatives, and the election
of officers, meets every five years. We have no rules of rota-
tion, which is both a curse and a blessing. It allows us to
keep good people, and it also makes it difficult to get rid of
those who are too old or past their usefulness.

As Chairman of the North American branch, there wasn't
then a whole lot to do. The branch wasn't very important,
and frankly, neither was the organization. The WJC was not
at all well known in America, and though it was better known
in Canada, it was not busily engaged; the Canadian Jewish
Congress, which had had an enormously important role to
play in the lives of Canadian Jews during and immediately
after World War II, was losing its primacy. Nahum himself
was known in the United States, for he had lived in New York
from 1939 to 1959, had been very active in Jewish affairs,
and had formed the Conference of Presidents of Major Jewish
Organizations at the behest of John Foster Dulles, who had
gotten fed up with the president of each Jewish organization
demanding to see him every time something happened
between the United States and Israel. I guess Nahum's am-
bition had been to get all the organizations in the Diaspora
under one roof—his—which might have given him more

leverage in Israel to promote his personal views, especially regarding the question of peace. To that end, he had also founded an organization that included both B'nai B'rith and the WJC to hold dialogues with the Catholic Church, called IJCIC, the International Jewish Committee on Interreligious Conferences. When Nahum had returned to Europe, however, and taken up residence in Paris, the WJC had lost most of its local importance. Which explains why there wasn't much to do.

Nahum's greatest claim to fame was his accomplishments with the Conference on Jewish Material Claims Against Germany, which he chaired. This had been founded in 1945 by the World Zionist Organization and its partner, the Jewish Agency for Palestine. It still operates today, and tries to get help for the concentration camp survivors who lived behind the Iron Curtain, and who received nothing while they lived under communism. It also conducted serious negotiations with what was East Germany, which never paid reparations to Israel, as West Germany had. The Claims Conference, although it was mostly a one-man show—Father also was slightly involved—had negotiated on behalf of the State of Israel and the Jewish people for reparations from the Federal Republic of Germany. His opposite number had been Konrad Adenauer, *der alte*, and the two had had a great meeting of the minds. As of today, some $73 billion have left Germany to take care of survivors of the camps, to provide for victims of atrocities, and to build the infrastructure of the State of Israel. There were huge arguments between David Ben-Gurion and Menachem Begin as to whether or not Israel should accept German reparations. Begin took what he thought was the high ground, maintaining that there was no way to pay for one Jewish life, let alone 6 million. Ben-Gurion took the more pragmatic view that there was no way the Germans could be forgiven their crimes—but in the meantime, Israel desperately needed the money. As they might say in Talmud, Ben-Gurion's view prevailed.

The World Jewish Congress received a tiny share of the Claims Conference money, and I assumed that it was reasonably well financed. Upon assuming a leadership role, I was to discover that this was not the case.

Nahum's influence was declining with his advancing years—he was in his early eighties—and there was a perceived need to have him step down. The two main actors on that stage were Philip Klutznick and Sol Kanee. Phil held the personal title of Ambassador, for the role he had played in the United Nations under Ambassador Adlai Stevenson, and he had been President of B'nai B'rith, the parent organization of the Anti-Defamation League and of Hillel, which serves on campuses in the United States and Canada and, lately, Israel, Russia, and Ukraine. He was a well-known figure nationally, but more particularly in Chicago, where he had lived since he was a young man. At this time, the early 1970s, he was Chairman of the WJC Board of Governors. Sol Kanee—his given name was Solomon, but when he'd hung up his lawyer's shingle in Melville, Saskatchewan, and had wanted gold lettering for his name, he'd found that Solomon was much too expensive, and so had it changed—had been a good friend of Father's, and was that rare person who could befriend two generations, for he has also been a close friend and adviser to my brother, Charles, and to me. He had succeeded to the presidency of the Canadian Jewish Congress, was also a good friend to Nahum, and an officer of the WJC.

I had no argument with the contention that Nahum was too old for the job of President, nor did I have any intention of succeeding him. Phil wanted the job? Phil got the job. We persuaded Nahum to step down, and after all these years, Nahum did not seem averse to the idea. He said, and I quote, "I have the best title in the world—Nahum Goldmann." At a meeting of the General Council of the World Jewish Congress, which has the power to act for the Plenum, and is necessary with a change of presidents, Phil Klutznick was duly elected, and Nahum's long reign ended. It was 1977, and because I had some influence with the Carter White House, I managed to get the President to address the group during the two-day meeting in Washington.

Phil Klutznick never really had a chance to show what he could do as President of the WJC, however. In 1978, about six months after his election to the presidency of the WJC, President Carter asked him to be the Secretary of Commerce. I'm sure he thought that naming Phil to a Cabinet position would help with the Jewish vote in the upcoming election. Phil made it a condition of accepting the Cabinet position that he could remain as President of the WJC, but in the meantime someone would have to be at the helm.

My first choice was Arthur Hertzberg, past President of the American Jewish Congress, whose opinions on the basic issues were similar to those Nahum had held, and with which I was comfortable. However, the World Zionist Organization was our most important member and had veto power over the selection of the President of the WJC, which they exercised with Rabbi Hertzberg, a man with an Orthodox upbringing who had become a Conservative Jew out of conviction. Menachem Begin was Israel's Prime Minister, and it was well known that he detested Hertzberg's views on the Likud's settlements; Hertzberg had written often and scathingly that such activity was contrary to a peaceful settlement of the Israel-Arab conflict. The WZO, then and now, was very conscious of the attitude of the *rosh ha memshala* (head of government). Sol Kanee was very active in trying to resolve the issue of the presidency, and he kept looking at me, and I kept shaking my head no. Finally, using his creative skills, Sol dreamed up the following scheme. The organization would be run by the heads of the four branches extant at the time—North America, Latin America, Europe, and Israel—and I, representing the most populous one, would be the "Convener." I asked what that meant, and Sol said cutely that when we needed to have a meeting, I would convene it. I agreed to so do until the next plenary session.

Enter Israel Singer. An ordained Orthodox rabbi, a Ph.D., and a professor—he had taught at Bar Ilan University in Israel and at Brooklyn College—Israel was active in the WJC New York office. He took hold of me and began to dream a dream about Soviet Jewry. All of my grandparents had come from there, and I felt, deep down inside, an obligation to do something for those Jews still there. He told me about their sorrowful plight, and sold me on the fact that, since the WJC's members included all the countries behind the Iron Curtain except the USSR, we were in a better position than any other group to try to improve the lot of Soviet Jewry. We spoke many hours, and I was entranced by this man, one of the brightest I had ever met, as well as the most hardworking, driven, and at the same time, nicest.

There had been a man working for the WJC in Paris called Armand Kaplan. This fellow had managed to convince Nahum Goldmann that he was making progress in getting him an invitation to Moscow, and he was wont to have lunches and dinners in fancy restaurants, always with someone codenamed by a letter of the alphabet. I believe that Armand enjoyed many a good meal that way. Nahum was so desperate for that invitation that he was easily beguiled. We decided to try a more direct approach.

Singer, who in the past had accompanied both Goldmann and Klutznick to meetings with Soviet Ambassador Anatoly Dobrynin, took me to the Soviet embassy in Washington. I was fairly impressed with the embassy. It was cold, with a ferocious-seeming security apparatus. Eventually, someone came downstairs and escorted us up to the room where we were to meet with the Ambassador. The room was fairly attractive, done in Russian "Peter the Great" style, with a couple of pictures by mediocre Russian artists, and a couch surrounded by comfortable overstuffed chairs and a coffee table in the middle. Anatoly Dobrynin was a big man, and he used his size much the way Lyndon Johnson had, to be slightly overbearing. His voice was deep and his English was almost perfect, although accented. He was then the dean of the diplomatic corps, having been Ambassador longer than anyone else. At this first meeting, he was very cordial, and

I felt that we just might be able to do business together. Singer did most of the talking, asking for the release of refuseniks, and I watched Anatoly and decided that he was a fairly decent man. One thing I learned was that he and his wife were the "parents" of their granddaughter. Due to family problems, he and his wife had decided to rear the girl themselves.

After President Gorbachev recalled Dobrynin to Moscow in March 1987, because of his special expertise on Washington, I always visited him when I was in Moscow. I believe his understanding of the United States, and of America's position on Jews in general and Israel in particular, helped us achieve our goal for Soviet Jewry.

In the early months of 1979, the WJC muddled along. From Singer's standpoint, I was the senior officer, and he kept after me for organizational direction and for my signature on bank loans to keep the doors open. The financial situation was unsound. We had many more expenditures than we had income, and a growing debt. The money Nahum had secured from the Germans had been all but spent, without any serious attempt at fund-raising, and there were no new sources of revenue. This situation was untenable, and I slowly started to right the tilting ship.

At a meeting of the Governing Board in Amsterdam,

the Nahum Goldmann Medal was presented to Helmut Schmidt. This was a great evening for Nahum, and I, as senior officer, made the actual presentation. Phil Klutznick was there as Secretary of Commerce, and when I told him that I intended to run for the office of President, he heartily agreed with my decision.

Not long after, Phil came over for an early lunch. I iterated that I was serious about becoming President. This time, I told him he had to decide whether he wanted me to run. He said that he enjoyed being a Cabinet officer.

"Yes," I replied, "but suppose you lose the election."

"Edgar, we're not going to lose!"

"Yes, but, Phil, supposing you do, would you like to resume at the WJC?"

"No, Edgar," he said. "I've got books to write and books to read and I want to spend time with my Ethel [his wife of forever] and my grandchildren at the farm."

"Are you absolutely sure, Phil?"

"Yes."

We all know what happened to Carter in the election of 1980—but Phil was true to his word.

The first step was to get rid of the title "Convener," and have myself elected as acting President of the WJC. I remember the event clearly. At a meeting of the Executive

Committee in London in April 1979, Phil Klutznick proposed me, and then everyone in the room, all twenty or so, one after the other, commented on articles I'd written for the press, in which I'd expressed my lack of total support for some decisions made by the Likud government of Israel. Those articles had been critical of the settlements policies referred to before—I thought like Nahum Goldmann and Arthur Hertzberg on that issue, but I hadn't been vetoed, because the name Bronfman had a certain panache, even with Prime Minister Begin. After the last person had said what he had to say, I suggested that we bring the matter to a vote.

"Aren't you going to respond?" someone asked.

"No," I answered. I saw no reason to defend myself. I had always felt that I had a right, perhaps even a duty, to disagree with the Israeli government when I thought it wrong, and in danger of losing the support of the American government and of the American people should Israel abandon the high moral ground. I also didn't respond to the arrows flung my way about publishing those views in the *New York Times*. The point was that to criticize in the Israeli press was one thing, but in America it might reflect disunity, and hence weakness. There may have been something to that argument, but if it weren't in the *New York Times*, then nobody in Israel would pay any attention.

I was unanimously elected acting President. It wasn't a clear mandate, since I had yet to be elected by the full Plenum, but it was a pretty good beginning.

Next, we had to do something about the debt, the revenues, and the direction we were taking. Some thrusts would have to be made judiciously. Leon Dulzin, the Chairman of the Executive Committee of the World Zionist Organization and of the Jewish Agency—these two posts are always filled by the same person—had made it clear that he thought the WJC should restrict itself to the fight against anti-Semitism. I took that to mean that he wanted us to stay away from the peace process and Soviet Jewry, which at the time I was loath to do. As for the debt, my extremely generous brother undertook to help me retire it, with the help of my sister Phyllis. We started a direct-mail campaign, which continues to be very successful, and in 1986, a gala dinner at the Waldorf Astoria in New York raised a significant amount of money.

Israel Singer's, and my, first act was to try to strengthen our relationships with the Jewish communities in the Western Hemisphere. We traveled throughout Latin America, with me working for Seagram during the day, and for the World Jewish Congress during the evening.

Then the time came for me to go to Jerusalem to be examined by the political parties that could influence my election as "full" President. In dealing with Israelis, whether government officials, members of the Knesset, or ordinary citizens, one must bear in mind that many, if not most, look at life differently from Jews who live in the Diaspora.

In presenting myself as a candidate for the presidency of the WJC or of any other volunteer organization, I had to recognize as well, as incredible as it may seem, that in Israel, everything elective follows the pattern of the Knesset. If a party has 4 percent of the Knesset seats, it then has that same proportion within local volunteer organizations. I am not sure how Prime Minister Begin felt about me. He was reputed not to like rich men. He probably knew that, while I have never proclaimed allegiance to any Israeli party, I, like so many others, had grown up as a Jew during the Labor Party's dominance of the political scene.

Let me amend the term "dominance": When I first went to Israel, I was amazed that all hotels had kosher facilities, including separate milk and meat service and eating areas. I was told that this had been the deal that Dr. Josef Burg, head of the National Religious Party, had made with Ben-Gurion so that the Labor Party would have a majority. This coalition had ruled Israel from the creation of the state until Begin's victory in 1977.

I submitted myself to meetings with four or five political parties, and was yelled at by some and overpraised by others, but in January 1981 I was elected President of the World Jewish Congress. Raya Yaglom, the President of

WIZO, the Women's International Zionist Organization, was an early and staunch supporter; she castigated my critics, saying they should consider themselves lucky that someone young and with leadership potential was willing to do the job.

———

It is probably no longer true, but for years, many looked upon me as Nahum Goldmann's disciple. His thoughts were supposedly mine. I did not fight such an image. I adored him and respected him deeply, but we differed in our approaches and in our backgrounds. He was a European Jew, born in the Pale of Settlement, and a little chary of brash American Jews. I am a transplanted Canadian, an American citizen, perceived to be a successful businessman, with all that implies. I live in New York City, where Jews are unbelievably secure, and am too young to have any real memories of the horrors of the Holocaust.

As Nahum grew older, he became more and more a maverick. His instructions to me were that the WJC must always remain independent of the Israeli government. The theme in the books he wrote, mostly in French, was that time was not on Israel's side, and that the Israelis were foolishly letting opportunities for a peaceful settlement slip by. I did not always agree with him. I understood then, as I do now, that there are a great many Arabs who are implacably opposed to

Israel's existence, and that peace would come only when the conditions were right.

At a meeting of the WJC Executive Committee in Paris, which came very soon after the Israeli march on Lebanon in the fall of 1982, Goldmann, Klutznick, and former French Premier Mendes-France issued a joint statement condemning the incursion. The statement would have been better timed had they issued it after Arik (Ariel) Sharon had marched all the way to Beirut. But early on it was not the thing to do. The original purpose of the military operation was to secure the immediate border between Lebanon and Israel, and see to it that no more rockets would be aimed and fired at the Israeli settlements in the northern Galilee. I doubt that even Prime Minister Begin knew what his Defense Minister was planning for the Palestinians in the D.P. camps outside Beirut.

To make certain that the World Jewish Congress was in no way responsible for the statements of two of its past presidents, our Executive Committee denounced this statement. That noon, I went to Nahum's for lunch—just the two of us. I was seated with drink in hand when Nahum spoke. "So you denounced me?"

I thought for a moment, decided I had no reason to say otherwise, and nodded.

He laughed. "I would have, too, if I had been you."

CHAPTER 4

SOVIET JEWRY

Slowly but surely, I began to focus on the plight of Soviet Jewry. Nahum had set a fine example. He often said that we had lost 6 million Jews to Hitler, and he was not going to lose another 3 million (no one had any real information on just how many) Jews in the Soviet Union. My father's family had come from what was then Bessarabia, now Moldova, and my mother's folks were from Ukraine, and because of their sacrifices, my generation of Bronfmans was where it was. I had come to feel an obligation to those whose grandparents had not made that arduous journey.

Nahum Goldmann had hoped and prayed that he would be invited to Moscow, but he never was. In terms of their objectives, the authorities there had viewed him as powerless. I, being an American and perceived as an important business figure, had a better shot at a breakthrough.

I inherited one organizational bonanza from Nahum's regime: the membership of the Jewish communities in Eastern Europe. With the exception of the Soviet Union, Jewish communities from every country behind the Iron Curtain were represented. This gave us an opportunity to practice an *ostpolitik* of our own.

Together, Singer and I dreamed of changing life for the Jews in the Soviet Union. We formed a new strategy, which we dubbed a two-track thrust. The first track was to create plenty of noise—chaining to embassies and general *shraying*—which would put us in position for the second track, bargaining with Moscow: If you do this, we will stop the demonstrations. We worked closely with the World Union of Jewish Students, because that group always could be counted on to create a "rally" when one was needed. Nahum had been totally against demonstrations, saying you could not treat a superpower that way. He was so adamant that he even avoided Brussels I, where the whole world had gathered to protest the plight of Soviet Jewry.

We established a credo. Our goals, derived from Nahum's, were threefold. We wanted the release of all Prisoners of

Zion, people incarcerated for no other reason except their openly expressed desire to emigrate to Israel.

We wanted the Soviet government to allow all those who wanted to emigrate to Israel to do so freely.

We wanted those who remained in the Soviet Union to be able to lead dignified lives as Jews: to be able to pray, to teach their children their traditions (or to have them taught, because after seventy years of communism, so few Jews knew anything), and to be proud of their Judaism rather than having to hide it.

This third goal included the teaching of Hebrew, which was forbidden—people like Joseph Begun were jailed for such activity—and the right to practice all forms of Judaism, including the right to mikvahs, kosher facilities, the availability of kosher food preparation, rabbis, and Jewish education in Jewish schools, all despite the Communist Party's ban against any religious activity whatsoever. Indeed, in working for the rights of Jews, it was important that the Russian Orthodox Church also win concessions from the government.

Our third goal differed from that of the Israelis. The Israelis were not interested in the rights of Jews who chose to stay in the Soviet Union. They only wanted Jews to leave the Soviet Union and come to Israel. To this day, I believe that everyone should be able to live anywhere he or she chooses. And let's be fair: most of the Jews who wanted to leave the USSR preferred to go to the United States or Canada. They didn't want to go to Israel and be good Jews; they wanted to go to the West and leave their Jewishness behind them. This issue was divisive in the Jewish world then and was not to be resolved until much later, first when the Soviets agreed that all Jews could leave, and then when the Soviet Union collapsed. When that happened, the Soviet Jews were no longer political refugees, and so were no longer able to come to the United States except on a quota system, just like all other would-be immigrants. The gates to America narrowed to an annual limit of 40,000 immigrants. But this was a long way off.

In the meantime, there were heated arguments between those Jews who thought that Soviet Jews should go wherever they pleased, and those who thought they all ought to go to Israel. The Hebrew word for the sin of not going to Israel is *noshira*, and at its worst, well over 90 percent of Soviet Jewish émigrés were not going to Israel.

I remember an incident in Margaret Thatcher's office. We had called upon her to persuade President Gorbachev to "let my people go," and Neil Bradman, Chairman of the British Soviet Jewry movement, asked Mrs. Thatcher to request

Gorbachev to release only these Jews who wanted to go to Israel. I quickly moved in, much to her satisfaction, and repudiated that statement. We must always keep to the high ground, I said. To make a request like that would only antagonize the Soviets—on two fronts. We would be asking them to make Israel stronger, while the Arabs were their clients, and also to do our work for us.

There's one story I love to tell about Mrs. Thatcher, a woman I admire enormously. I was invited by the Chairman of United Biscuit, now Sir Hector Laing, to the annual dinner he used to give in his London flat for the Prime Minister's birthday. It was a very small group, eight in all, including Mrs. T. and her husband, Denis. Knowing of the dinner months in advance, I kept my eye open for a suitable gift. One day, thumbing through the *New Yorker*, I came across a cartoon that featured a rather plain girl sitting on a couch and a sincere, not-at-all-charismatic man speaking earnestly. The caption read, "Marry me, dear. I love you more than any other woman, except of course for my mother and Margaret Thatcher." After dinner, I presented it to her, as others had done with their gifts, and she looked at it, howled with laughter, and said, "Denis, I know exactly where I am going to put this." I took a chance, but she has a great sense of humor.

To attain our goals, we knew we would have to go to Moscow. We envisioned escalating to higher and higher circles, because we would make our case so compelling that we would have to be passed along—ever upward. (I was to learn a lot more about the difficulties when I finally got a visa to go to the Soviet Union.)

This all seemed like such a tall order, such a monumental task, that in speaking to groups, I would often use a line from the Talmud: "You are not called upon to complete the work, yet you are not free to evade it." You had to put forth your best efforts, and believe that even if you couldn't finish the job, others coming after you might.

Ambassador Anatoly Dobrynin had repeatedly told me that if I would travel as a businessman, he could give me a visa to Moscow "right now" (meaning without referring the request to Moscow), but I kept insisting that I would go only as President of the WJC.

Finally, in a meeting on May 13, 1980, he told me he had recommended that I receive a visa, and lo and behold, I got it. I am not sure what accounted for the change, but this we all knew: the climate for helping Soviet Jewry improved or deteriorated depending on the relationship between the superpowers. Although we knew nothing about it at the time, the Soviets were getting desperate for trade with the West.

I was not surprised when President Gorbachev recalled
Anatoly Dobrynin as Ambassador to the United States. He
wanted him to be Secretary of the Central Committee for
International Affairs. If I had been the General Secretary of
the Communist Party of the Soviet Union, desperately in
need of better trade relations with the United States, I too
would have sought out the person who knew the most about
the United States, and I would have kept him near at hand.
Without question, that person was Dobrynin.

Before going to the USSR as the World Jewish Congress president, it seemed only prudent to test the climate
to see what kind of welcome I might expect. To scout out
the lay of the land, I sent Bill Friedman (who now directs
much of the charitable efforts of Seagram and its foun-
dations) and Israel Singer in December 1982. Within a
couple of days they called me from Russia to tell me point-
blank not to come, because the atmosphere was so very hostile. Georgiy Arbatov, the Director of the Institute for the
United States and Canada, had been insulting, and had actually thrown an ashtray at Singer as their conversation became overheated. Friedman and Singer were taking a chance
with their advice, because there might not have been a next
time, but I trusted their instincts and stayed home. It was
clear that the Soviets had miscalculated. They had figured

that I wanted to go as desperately as Nahum Goldmann had.

Enter Jim Giffen, President and Chief Operating Officer of the U.S./USSR Trade and Economic Council, or USTEC, on whose executive committee I had served. The joint CEOs on this committee were a prominent American business-man, originally Donald Kendall of PepsiCo—and a Soviet bureaucrat (all Soviet members were totally pro forma and nameless). Jim was eager to increase trade between the super-powers, and he figured, probably correctly, that there would be no most-favored-nation treatment for the USSR as long as the terms of the Jackson/Vanik amendment were not met. Without MFN, there could be no meaningful increase in U.S./USSR trade.

Jackson/Vanik had been stuck onto the 1976 Foreign Aid Bill in order to motivate the Soviets to be more reasonable in their treatment of those Soviet Jews who wished to emi-grate. The legislation, which carries the names of Senator Henry Jackson (D-Washington) and Representative Charles Vanik (R-Ohio), states (it's still on the books) that the Soviet Union and other listed Communist countries could not be granted MFN unless the President certified that they allowed free emigration. Alternatively, the President could waive this restriction on a yearly basis, but that waiver was subject to a congressional overrule, which was, in turn, subject to a presidential veto.

Even with Jackson/Vanik, it might have been possible to negotiate the departure of perhaps 60,000 Jews a year, but Jackson/Vanik supporters insisted on the principle, not just the numbers. They were probably correct. I now believe that both the Israelis and the State Department took this position, which I now like to call the "high road." I say "now," because many times, looking at the numbers—less than 1,000 a year for so many years—Singer and I would moan about the number that might have been.

Jim Giffen and I became friends, and he succeeded in getting me to the proper echelon of people in Moscow. I then set out to convince the Soviets that Edgar Bronfman and the World Jewish Congress were the keys to their getting most-favored-nation status.

I had visited Moscow once before, in 1963. I was then thirty-four, John F. Kennedy was President of the United States, and Nikita Khrushchev was General Secretary of the Communist Party of the Soviet Union. The trip had been arranged by *Time* magazine, and was the first of many *Time* tours that took business executives to all parts of the world.

These many years later, I still have sharp memories of

that first trip to Moscow. We started in Washington with briefings, including a session with the President. Kennedy seemed very assured, and very contemplative. I am not sure what his regard was for Harry Luce and Time, Inc.—and my impression was that he was going through the motions and was not overly impressed with either the group or its mission. Most Presidents rather dislike businessmen getting involved with foreign policy. Former Ambassador Llewelyn "Tommy" Thompson told us that the Soviets would assume they were talking to the real power in America, because they were dealing with a group of high-powered business leaders. He also told us that we could probably do whatever we wanted to do while we were there, but to remember that there would probably be pictures!

We had no idea how they would treat us, but once we arrived, it was clear they were going to give us the best treatment. I have since learned that the Soviets didn't always keep people in the dark out of malice. The bureaucracy just had a terrible time dealing with the unexpected. Its inefficiency was built in, as was its instinct to pass the buck, since it was always safest to do nothing—there was absolutely no reward for being innovative.

The airport had been cleared out for our arrival, and we were served local champagne and brandy in the presence of a display of jewelry, which we were encouraged to purchase. Then, after a minimum of fuss with formalities, Chaika and Zil limousines whisked us to the Sovietskaya Hotel, which, we were told, was always reserved for high-ranking diplomats from the Eastern Bloc and Communists from Third World countries. The service was terrific (one's wash was done daily), but the cuisine left much to be desired. At breakfast, one of our group asked for a four-minute egg, and was served four one-minute eggs (we learned that the only thing the staff understood about eggs was "omelet"). There was no shortage of caviar, but everything else was terrible. The lamb looked all right, but you couldn't cut into it with a ratcheted knife. There were cucumbers and some tomatoes, but no other fruits or vegetables.

We also learned about "photocracy." When our group was ushered into Chairman Khrushchev's presence, we encountered a mass of television cameras and still photographers. At one point, hearing the press ordering us about, Nikita Khrushchev said, "You see, it's not true that I run things in Russia. The photographers do." He was very impressive during our interview with him. Richard Clurman, then chief of correspondents for Time, Inc., had told us, "For a relevant public purpose, there is no such thing as a rude question: only a question rudely asked." Premier Khrushchev answered questions for more than three hours, sitting alone except for his interpreter, who had an American accent, and who, we found out later, had been brought up in Washington, the son of a former diplomat. Khrushchev showed himself to be a talented politician, unbelievably sure of himself. His stature was unimpressive, he was not at all attractive, and he seemed a bit crude—perhaps unpolished is a kinder word—but he had a great command of the facts and figures, and not one question seemed to present him with any difficulty.

During an intermission at the Bolshoi Theater, I used brash humor to score points with our regular Intourist guide sitting on my left, as well as with the head of the Intourist group, a Party member, sitting on my right. I asked the Party member to point out where Stalin used to sit. It was fairly obvious that he had probably sat in the empty box down front.

Why did I want to know? she asked. "Look here," I replied, "Comrade Khrushchev has instructed you to answer all our questions, and I expected an answer, and not a question."

She pointed to the empty loge quite close to the stage.

I thanked her, and said that I wished to go there forthwith and take a seat. She turned white as a sheet, and again asked why.

"Because," I said, "Comrade Khrushchev has instructed

you to take us anywhere we want to go, and that's where I want to go."

She sighed resignedly, and said, "Oh, very well," still insisting on the reason for this outrageous request.

I told her the reason was simple. Under their ancient and presumably honorable ideology, I, as a capitalist businessman, was an oppressor of the masses.

"Is that not so?" I asked her.

She acknowledged that this was so.

I continued: "Is it not a fact that Comrade Khrushchev has recently announced that Stalin had been an oppressor of the masses?"

She acknowledged that this, too, was accurate.

"Well," I concluded, "I just want to sit in my rightful place—in the oppressor's box." But then, much to her relief, I smiled and relented.

(More brash humor: I once was asked, "What would have happened if, instead of John F. Kennedy, Nikita Khrushchev had been assassinated?" I confessed that I didn't have the faintest idea, and the answer came back, "Ari Onassis would not have married Mrs. Khrushchev.")

I vividly recall Khrushchev's rudeness, not to us, but to his own colleagues, a kind of disdainful brutishness. During a conversation about selling Russian vodka in the United States and Seagram's 7 Crown in the USSR, I asked, "Mr. Chairman, with whom should I discuss this further?" He gestured imperiously toward Anastas Mikoyan, a Politburo member, and sneered, "Him." No mention of a name, let alone a title. Years later, I realized that this rude man had probably made it possible for Gorbachev to attack Stalinism. Had he not led the way, it might have been even harder for the average Soviet citizen to accept the truth.

The first trip took place many years before I became immersed in the work of the World Jewish Congress. At that time, I was only casually aware of my Jewishness, and had made no attempt to learn anything about Soviet Jews. I had not heard of refuseniks. I did know that the practice of religion was proscribed, but I felt that it was not particularly anti-Semitic, since that proscription applied to all religions.

My next trip to the Soviet Union was in 1968, when I was, for a short period of time, chairman of MGM. The United States Information Agency wanted us to show *2001: A Space Odyssey* at the Moscow Film Festival, and then take it to the other Eastern European countries, all while Neil Armstrong and company were headed for the moon, and before they landed. To do this on commercial airlines would have been impossible, so I asked my friend Jack Valenti, President of the Motion Picture Association, to obtain permission for us to

bring the Seagram airplane to Moscow. This was very difficult, but he managed to do so. Our party stayed at the 1,000-
room, three-blocks-square Rossiya Hotel. It was so huge and
so badly planned that one could get lost trying to go from one
section to another. In fact, our flight attendant did get lost
the next morning when we departed, and was crying hope-
lessly when by chance someone in the group recognized her
and showed her the way out.

When we arrived at the airport to leave, we were given a terrific taste of bureaucracy at its worst. The pleasant Intourist
guide who was in charge of our group seemed to be waiting
for something, while we just wanted to board our aircraft
and leave. So I asked her, "What are we waiting for?" Her
answer was a patient, "First your airplane will be announced,
and then we will go to the immigration counter for passport
checks." "But, my dear, it is a private airplane." At this, she
looked nonplussed, so I walked her to the edge of the floor,
where we could see the tarmac, and our airplane between two
others. "Do you see that little airplane between those two
Ilyushins?" I asked. "Oh, yes, a very nice airplane." "Fine,"
I said, "that's our airplane. Now, who is going to announce
it?" "I don't know, perhaps the pilot," she said, and burst into
tears. I then pointed out to her that the pilots were standing at
the bottom of the embarkation ladder at the airplane, and

she cried a little harder. Fortunately, Seagram's chief pilot, Donald Jorgensen, saw us and, sensing that there was a problem, made his way to our sides. He said, "We're ready to go." She exclaimed with glee, "Your plane has been announced."

Off we went to the next hurdle. A uniformed man whose hairline almost reached his bushy eyebrows asked, in a bored voice, for our tickets. I tried to explain that we didn't have any tickets, we had our own airplane. He had a stamp in his hand, and we had nothing for him to stamp. That just would not do. I wished that I had had the foresight to pick up some PanAm ticket envelopes, but in any event the Intourist guide finally persuaded him to let us through. When we got to Immigration, Chief Pilot Jorgensen's passport was in the custody of the police officer who had escorted the crew to the airplane. He excused himself, disappeared, and then found his way to the aircraft by the same subterranean method he had used to find us. The whole thing took an hour and a half.

When we arrived in Warsaw, our next stop, we were met at the aircraft itself, right on the runway, by embassy cars. Someone took care of our passports and we were whisked off to the Ambassador's residence. And so it was in the rest of Eastern Europe. Only Moscow was abysmally ignorant of how to deal with private aircraft. I don't believe anyone was being especially mean in the USSR, it's just that when you didn't know what to do, you either passed the buck or did nothing—but never did you improvise!

In 1987, at the time of my first official visit as President of the World Jewish Congress, Mikhail Gorbachev was General Secretary of the CPSU, and had been since March 1985. It didn't take long to find that the Soviets hadn't really changed since my 1963 trip, when Khrushchev had asked why we didn't buy more from his country, and I had answered, "You don't make anything we want." When he had said, "Well, then, tell us what you want and we'll make it," I, looking at him somewhat askance, had replied, "It doesn't work that way." How can you teach free-market economics in thirty seconds?

Now, here it was, twenty-four years later, and except for vodka, they still didn't make consumer products that could be sold in any Western country.

My first official contact with the Communist Party of the Soviet Union was with Mr. Vadim Zagladin, who was acting head of the International Bureau, known earlier as the Comintern. The meeting was held in the Kremlin (I gather under instruction from Mikhail Gorbachev), which site gave the meeting added weight. We discussed, among other things, Meir Kahane, Soviet refuseniks, our three goals, the world situation, and American politics. The discussions were polite but cool.

Zagladin pretended he didn't speak English, and the translation took much time, which gave one time to think. (A few years later, I again met Zagladin in Dobrynin's CPSU headquarters office. His English was perfect! When I remarked on this, he laughed as if to say, "Now it's different, we trust you.")

While the results were not terrific, I gradually came to understand that, with this very suspicious group of people, the name of the game was building trust. The meeting with Zagladin was the first of many with officials at higher and higher levels, which eventually led to my meeting with President Gorbachev in December of 1990.

Every time Israel Singer and I met with Dobrynin in Washington, we took along the list of refuseniks, and focused on one or two special cases. Each time we brought up the issue, Dobrynin would say, "As soon as I give you one, you will ask for two more," and we would readily agree, saying we were dedicated to getting them all. He would laugh, but occasionally we were successful.

Our first success was with Joseph Mendelevitch, one of the Leningrad hijackers who had tried unsuccessfully to steal a Soviet aircraft and divert it to Israel. The group had been betrayed by an informer and they all had received twelve-year sentences. Mendelevitch was an interesting man, who had known nothing of Judaism until he had gone to prison, where he taught himself Hebrew. We arranged for his release after he had served some ten years of the sentence, and Israel Singer met him in Vienna in February 1981. All Jews who left the Soviet Union went to Vienna before traveling to their next destination. Israel taught Mendelevitch how to lay tefillin, and stayed with him until his plane left for Tel Aviv.

On his first trip to New York one year later, Mendelevitch stopped in my office. He asked me if I was the man who had gotten him out of the Soviet Union. Trying to be modest, I hemmed and hawed a bit. Israel Singer, who had brought him in, said, "This is Mr. Bronfman, the President of the World Jewish Congress. He is the man who arranged for your release." Thereupon, Mendelevitch reached into a shabby briefcase and brought out a white skullcap. He explained that he had made it in prison using a chicken bone as a needle and threads from his thin robe. This he gave to me. I was overwhelmed. I knew I couldn't keep it, and on my next trip to Jerusalem, I gave it to Teddy Kollek so it would have a permanent home in the Israel Museum.

In March of 1987, I went to Moscow with Morris Abram, who was then the President of the American Conference on

Soviet Jewry, and also the Chairman of the Presidents' Conference. He was astonished at my contacts, and delighted to
visit Anatoly Dobrynin, among others, who told us that with
the exception of the "worst cases" and those who were known
to have knowledge of "state secrets," all the refuseniks would
be released in the coming year.

Many people in the Jewish community of New York disap-
proved of my dealings with the Soviets, on the grounds that
"you just couldn't trust them," and when we reported on our
conversation with Dobrynin, we were called "liars." Most of
these people were what I call professional Jews, hard-liners.
From professional jealousy or whatever reason, they refused
to believe the progress we were making. Not very long after, they had to confess that those two liars, Bronfman and
Abram, were telling the truth, when some 12,000 refuseniks
were released.

When Israel Singer brought Carmela Raiz to my office
in September 1988, I heard the story of a woman with two
children, whose husband was being hounded by a KGB officer with a personal grudge. Mrs. Raiz was very attractive, which might have been the reason for the hounding.
She and one of her sons were here in America, while her
husband and the other boy were still in the Soviet Union.
After listening to her tell her story, I promised to get

her husband and the other boy out. I knew that James Baker had already mentioned the Raiz problem to Foreign Minister Eduard Shevardnadze, but I also knew he couldn't make the subtle threat I could.

On my next trip to Moscow, on November 4, that same year, I met with Foreign Minister Shevardnadze, and presented him with a Russian translation of the letter I had written to everyone who mattered in Washington, advocating the repeal of Jackson/Vanik and the granting of MFN to the Soviet Union. He glanced through it quickly, told me how very important he considered it to be, and that he would personally show it to President Gorbachev. I then made my move.

I said there was a problem, however. His face fell. There was, I continued, a certain Mrs. Raiz, a most attractive woman, and as adamant as Avital Shcharansky in pursuing the release of her husband. Mrs. Shcharansky had been relentless in seeing and badgering everyone, including President Reagan, about her imprisoned husband, Anatoly, now Hebraized as Natan. I pictured Mrs. Raiz, asking Shevardnadze to contemplate her seeing everyone to whom I had sent the letter, every congressman, senator, and cabinet officer, and telling her sad tale. I went on to say that it was a distinct possibility that, when the matter came before the Congress of the United States, some representative or senator would raise the question of Zeev Raiz.

It would be a pity, I continued, and ridiculous for such a case to upset something so important to the Soviet Union and to the United States. I also told him that I knew that it was a personal vendetta, that I had met Mr. Raiz, and there was absolutely no way that he had secrets that could in any way affect the security of the USSR. Two weeks later, he was released.

Some time later, at a Hadassah dinner in my honor in May 1990, Mrs. Raiz told her story. She, of course, didn't know what I had said to Shevardnadze, so when it came my turn to speak I was able to round out the story.

As time went on, the meetings that made the real difference were with Eduard Shevardnadze. I also met a few times with Aleksandr Yakovlev, Gorbachev's closest confidant, but it was with Shevardnadze that real progress was made. Always accompanying me to these meetings was Israel Singer; often present was Steve Herbits, a Seagram Executive Vice President, in charge of public policy. Both Singer and Herbits took excellent notes, which made my work much easier.

Eduard Shevardnadze is a handsome man. Always well groomed, and given to three-piece suits, he had thinning but long wavy gray hair and blue eyes, and held himself erect and with great dignity. One of the politest men I met in Moscow, his courtesy was quite noble and sincere. At one time during a discussion, when I thought I hadn't made my point, and repeated it, he said, "Mr. Bronfman, we always pay great attention to everything you tell us."

One of our most exciting moments came in the spring of 1988, when the Soviet Foreign Minister told us what he would be proposing at the upcoming Helsinki Review meeting of the Committee for Security and Cooperation (CSCE) in Vienna. I had learned not to question the motivation when something like this happened. The Soviets had always been terribly shy about seeming weak. From our perspective, it had to be tied in with MFN and Jackson/Vanik.

We were totally amazed. The Soviet Union was about to agree to everything we had asked for, except free emigration. Laws granting religious freedom were to be enacted, and all rights for Jews living in the Soviet Union were to be secured. It was very clear that Shevardnadze was absolutely in charge of this arena in their Politburo's way of working, and that this was his personal decision. I am not sure even today whether or not it had been cleared with President Gorbachev.

The only request Shevardnadze made was that we not tell anyone until he presented his paper to the CSCE a few months hence. Nevertheless, from Moscow, we flew to Jerusalem on the *Seagram Gulfstream*, now in the *Guinness Book of Records* as the first-ever nonstop from the Soviet capital to the Israeli capital, where we reported what we had learned to Prime Minister Shamir. I'm sure Shevardnadze knew where we were going from Moscow, and I may even have mentioned it. Whatever the case, we also told those in Shamir's office that Foreign Minister Shevardnadze had requested we not tell anyone, but we had felt that the Prime Minister of Israel must know, and I strongly urged total discretion. Given the number of people present, I remain impressed with their self-imposed security. No one in the room breached this confidence. It is probable that neither Shamir nor the people in the room believed what they were hearing. Nobody was aware of the real situation in the Soviet Union and how desperate the place was becoming. They hadn't given in because we were such good guys, but because they'd known they were going to need us in the months and years ahead.

The proposals were duly made at CSCE, and the changes duly acted upon. On the evening of February 12, 1989, we attended an event at the Mikhoels Center, a Jewish theater in Moscow, which ushered in the new age of Jewish rights in the USSR. The press coverage was enormous—and Shevardnadze was out of town that evening. The foreign press made much of the event, but the Soviet press was very quiet. It wasn't until the next day, when I met with Mr. Shevardnadze, and he publicly said that he approved of what had happened the evening before, that the Soviet press acknowledged what the Western press had already reported. After my meeting with Shevardnadze, I was even interviewed from Moscow by CBS.

Mikvot (ritual baths) were suddenly allowed, and they were to be brought somewhat up to speed from their previous condition. Jewish schools were suddenly approved, and the teaching of Hebrew was no longer banned. Young Jewish kids were enrolled in these schools to get them prepared to make *aliyah*, and soon the flood of immigrants descended upon Israel. It was all wonderful, but being suspicious of the constant change in the power structure in Moscow, I began to arrange a visit with President Gorbachev, to try to make sure that the gates wouldn't be shut again.

It would be wrong to claim that the World Jewish Congress alone made the Soviets change their minds and let the Jews leave, but we were there at the right time, and we were able to show the Soviets what they had to do to be accepted as a civilized nation among civilized nations.

We also succeeded in convincing them that we held the keys to their most-favored-nation status. I once testified before Representative Lee Hamilton's House Committee on the subject, on January 17, 1990. While the testimony came some months after my meeting with Foreign Minister Shevardnadze and after he had announced the changes before the CSCE, the doors were not yet open to massive emigration. It was clearly time to apply more pressure. My statement was simple. The Soviet Union had not as yet complied with the provisions of the Jackson/Vanik amendment, and Jews were still not free to leave the Soviet Union. MFN should not be granted them. There were more Soviet embassy people in the room than American press. Although Jim Giffen tried to persuade the committee to grant MFN, it was my testimony that carried the day; the committee did not recommend MFN.

To understand why it took so much time, and so many trips, to accomplish our aims, even with the "new thinking" of President Gorbachev, one has to understand the Soviet Union as it was then. No one made a decision if he or she didn't have to. The established practice was to pass it on (or, in our case, pass "us" on) to a higher authority. For example, our experiences with Kharchev, the Chairman of the State Committee on Religion and Cults, changed markedly after we had seen his boss, Foreign Minister Shevardnadze. Kharchev confessed that he had never been in Shevardnadze's office! Suddenly, Kharchev was able to see Shevardnadze and receive his instructions directly. A happy man!

I was seen not only as a Jewish leader, but as an important business figure: one must remember that the Soviets (and former Soviets) still think that the Jews have undue influence, and that the real rulers in the West are those who run businesses. (By the way, they do not draw a distinction between ownership and professional management, which is sad, because this has only added to their difficulties in trying to make the transition from a command to a market economy.)

By 1990, as we had been passed along to higher and higher levels, we were told that we would probably meet President Gorbachev during our trip to Moscow in May, but by Friday morning, when no message confirming the meeting had come from the President's office, I decided we had been there long enough and that it was time to go home.

When we landed in Iceland to refuel, I received a message from my secretary, Maxine Hornung: we had an appointment for Saturday at two P.M. The message also said the President's office had tried to intercept our flight by radio communication while we were still over Soviet territory, but had been unable to do so. That didn't impress me; it sounded like sloppy staff work or an excuse. They had either waited too long or were too inefficient, or both.

I was tired. To turn around and land again in Moscow at two A.M., without hotel reservations, was neither inviting nor dignified, for that matter. I sent our apologies, and we kept heading west. When we finally met, in December 1990, I apologized to President Gorbachev once again and explained the great distances involved. He, of course, pooh-poohed the whole thing.

This time, all systems were working. President Gorbachev was confident to the point of being egotistical, made up for the cameras, and wearing an immaculately well tailored suit, with what looked like a white-on-white Sulka shirt (and, I was told, a corset)—a manicured picture of sartorial elegance. He had a nice smile, but his eyes were cold. He poured on the charm, but we were always aware of exactly who he was. He did this with body language and clever use of the interpreter, such as the occasional aside.

He loves to lecture, so he was difficult to talk to, but, to Steve Herbits's amazement, I did manage to hold my own. My mission was to ask for assurances that the gates that had been opened to allow Jews to emigrate to Israel would stay open.

I introduced the subject by telling him a joke I had heard that very morning in his foreign office:

Question: "What is the second language in Israel?"
Answer: "Hebrew."

He roared with laughter, and said, "Those are our people,

too." That really sounded like "my people" rather than "our people," or perhaps it was the imperial "we." I assured him that the brain drain was not so significant, and that when he put the Soviet economy back in shape, the Soviet Jews would return to do business. I am not sure he really cared; there were other things on his mind, such as the troubles with the Baltic nations.

But he was very definite in saying that the gates would stay open.

I don't know how in touch with events he was at this point. He had clearly decided to play with the conservatives for the moment and assured me that only he knew how to do this, that we liberals should not worry, because he had everything in hand. He clearly didn't have everything in hand in the Baltics, though. The three Baltic states, Lithuania, Estonia and Latvia, had been gobbled up by Stalin in his 1939 deal with Hitler. The United States had never recognized this perfidy, which might have had an emboldening effect on the Baltic peoples; when the Soviet Union began to crumble, that's when it started. To the world's horror, Soviet troops soon would fire on Lithuanian protesters. There would be much speculation as to whether or not Gorbachev had known in advance, had sanctioned these actions, or what role, if any, he had played.

I saw Foreign Minister Shevardnadze the next day. He had just resigned as Foreign Minister, and I asked him if there was any chance that he would reconsider his resignation, since not only his country but the world needed him.

He shook his head. His sad reply was that he now understood how a man could "self-immolate." His resignation was a protest against Gorbachev and his personality cult, which the Foreign Minister thought dangerous and undemocratic, and against what he considered "the onset of dictatorship." It was not a very long conversation, but it was very warm. He seemed to have a genuine affection for me and for my colleagues, Singer and Herbits, and as we shook hands to say good-bye, it seemed very different from other farewells of the past. Perhaps he foresaw the breakup of the Soviet Union. Perhaps he had already made up his mind to return to Georgia. I don't know, but I do know that he was through with Gorbachev and his role in helping guide the USSR.

———

As we progressed, Singer and I had developed two more goals, which were subsequently achieved despite the later dissolution of the entity called the Soviet Union. The first was that diplomatic relations be established between the Soviet Union and Israel, and the second that direct flights be established from the Soviet Union to Israel. The vast majority of immigrants made their way to Israel through Hungary.

In the spring of 1991, I pointed out to Aleksandr Yakovlev that the Soviets were losing the opportunity to earn millions in hard currency, because there were no direct flights. This conversation became very strange. We had been discussing my agenda, including direct flights, when Yakovlev suddenly sent everyone from the room, including my colleague Steve Herbits, leaving only his personal secretary to act as interpreter. Perhaps Gorbachev's closest confidant on matters of internal Soviet policy, Yakovlev was a man of little presence, medium height, and perhaps twenty pounds overweight, with thin black hair and a rather dour expression. For a moment, I considered protesting, and then decided to see what was coming. The ensuing conversation was interpreted only from Russian to English, because Aleksandr understood English perfectly. He had attended Columbia University and had spent six years as Soviet Ambassador to Canada.

He asked if there had been a meeting in Jerusalem of the major Jewish men of wealth, and if it was true that they had decided not to extend any credit to the Soviet Union.

I was nonplussed, and replied that the only meeting I knew about was one to collect money to house and find jobs for the hundreds of thousands of Jews who had emigrated to Israel from the Soviet Union, and that it would be impossible for a meeting such as the one he described to take place without my knowing about it.

This kind of suspicious thinking was straight from *The Protocols of the Elders of Zion*, the vicious forgery from czarist times that purported to show how the Jews intend to conquer the world.

He seemed satisfied with my answer, and then asked another question. "Would it be possible in your opinion for the Soviet Union to borrow fifteen billion dollars from the West to buy consumer goods from the West to sell to Soviet consumers?"

I replied that, while I thought the Soviet Union had at least that much credit, I did not think it would be a very good idea. It would be an attempt to buy themselves time to turn the economy around by bribing the Soviet consumers. I pointed out that, once they did that, they would have to keep on doing it, and soon they would run out of credit without having had any basic impact on the economy.

I suggested that a much better way to accomplish what he had in mind was to work with Western firms, to give them huge orders on the understanding that they build factories in the Soviet Union to produce those same consumer goods.

He thought about this and asked if that could possibly be done through joint ventures. I answered that this would depend on each negotiation, but it would be possible, as long as management control rested with the foreign investor. He, I'm afraid, was now lost. The concept was too foreign to him.

Yakovlev had spent considerable time in the West. I should have realized that if, after his years of experience in the United States and Canada, he still knew nothing about a market economy, then probably nobody in that entire country did. An exaggeration, perhaps, but not much of one.

I pursued the subject and said that I could put together a group of businessmen and bankers who could and would flesh out the approach I had just suggested. He was eager for this to be done (another example of passing the buck). Nothing, of course, ever came of it. The "of course" refers to the fact that Gorbachev really believed in socialism, and wasn't interested in transforming the Soviet Union into a market economy, even if he had known what that meant.

It was on one of these trips to the Soviet Union that I saw Israel Singer take a little book from his pocket, study it for about ten minutes, close it, and replace it in his pocket. Out of curiosity, I asked what that was he had just read. "That was the daily portion of Talmud," came the answer. Now even more curious, I asked, "What did it say?" Israel suggested that

I really didn't want to know. "I really do," I proclaimed. That's how my Jewish education started. What I basically learned from those sessions with Israel was how thousands of years ago, our sages and learned rabbis had interpreted the Bible, which they knew to be the fundamental thesis on Judaism, so as to teach people how to live with each other in justice. For instance, there is the interpretation of the biblical command that if an ox has gored three people, it must be destroyed. Talmud devotes much space on what should happen to the remains of the ox that have value. It might seem petty to us today, but this was a method of seeking justice, long before a system of torts had been developed.

I carried on in asking Singer about the portion of the day, and I kept getting more interested. Then I decided to read the Torah, starting from Genesis. That decision was put into effect on Simchat Torah of 1994. Israel Singer gave me the Stone edition, which has marvelous commentary, and when I had a problem, I would send an e-mail note to him, and then he would discuss the intricacies with me. Now I devote about two hours a week, but sometimes much more, depending on the time available. By the time of this writing, the end of January 1996, I am well into Kings I. I have had passionate discussions with both Israel Singer and Arthur Hertzberg about both King David and King Solomon, because the commentaries in the Judaica Books of the Prophets suggest that neither was a sinner, and I contend that in light of the commands of the Torah, both sinned. We haven't as yet totally reconciled, but I have now discovered one of the fun things about Torah study, the one-on-one process of argument, whose aim is to make both participants more understanding and a bit wiser.

———

In my travails with the Soviet Union, I must acknowledge the help of three people: Seweryn Bialer, Radomir Bogdanov, and Georgiy Arbatov.

Seweryn Bialer, now retired, was a professor at Columbia University, a historian of note, an eclectic scholar fascinated with military history, and at least at one time, probably the best-informed person in America on the Soviet Union. I first met Bialer when he expressed an interest in doing something for Soviet Jews. He had been born in Poland in the twenties, fought with the underground during World War II, when he was very young, and was captured and escaped a couple of times. He speaks fluent Russian, without a Polish accent, I'm told, and has many friends in the USSR. It was he who introduced me to Yakovlev and his principal assistant, Nikolai Shishlin, and to many other important people with whom he had connections.

When I first met Radomir Bogdanov, he was deputy to Georgiy Arbatov, the Director of the Institute for the United States and Canada, who had given Singer and Friedman so much trouble. Radomir had been a KGB general, and he must have done some pretty awful things, because every time anyone tried to get him a visa to the United States, both the FBI and the CIA stamped a great big NO on the application.

We became friendly because Radomir was the man who made arrangements, met the airplane, and on many occasions, delivered the refuseniks, such as Mendelevitch, the would-be Leningrad hijacker, and Ida Nudel. Ida Nudel, a devout and decent person, had been incarcerated because she supposedly knew state secrets, which was not true. She was the one refusenik whom all the women's groups in Jewish life insisted be freed; the persistent President of the Women's International Zionist Organization, Raya Yaglom, would never let a moment go by without insisting that I get Nudel out.

During one of our early trips, Radomir Bogdanov told me how important it was that America and the Soviet Union have better relations. I told him that I agreed, but that there were roadblocks, and he could help remove them. I gave him two names, Anatoly Shcharansky and Ida Nudel. I had nothing to do with the release of Shcharansky—President Reagan arranged that directly with Gorbachev at the Geneva Summit (one can only imagine how persistent Avital Shcharansky must have been, that the President of the United States would take up one man's name at a summit meeting) — but I did play a role in the release of Ida Nudel.

As I got to see and know more highly positioned people, Radomir was the one to arrange the meetings. Many trips later, we were having dinner at a Georgian restaurant. He had a lady with him, whom he introduced as his wife. I thought she might have looked Jewish, and the next morning, I asked him. He said, "No. I'm Jewish — my mother was a Jew." This was news indeed. The WJC arranged a trip to Israel for Radomir, and, wearing his *kipa*, he went around, buying this and that, having a wonderful time. When, not long ago, I told the poet Yevgeny Yevtushenko that Radomir had been a Jew, he, too, was astounded. Unfortunately, the poor fellow is now dead. He had a bad heart and we could never get him into this country for medical attention.

As for Georgiy Arbatov, since his first meeting with Singer and Friedman, he had changed and become a good friend of mine. I had many one-on-one meetings in his office, and we often dined together in Moscow and, since he traveled frequently to the United States, at my New York apartment. We also lunched occasionally with Anatoly Dobrynin at the

Soviet embassy in Washington. Arbatov once told me at a dinner in my home that his father was Jewish, and that the two of them had traveled together in Europe in 1938. From that trip, he had very distinct memories of how awful the Germans were being to the Jews. Arbatov was an important bureaucrat, and having him on our side made life easier in the bureaucratic maze of Moscow.

There is one story I'd like to tell, because it's so symptomatic of what went wrong in the Soviet Union, and probably still does. Our family had a controlling interest in a skate manufacturer called Bauer—top of the line. I thought it might be a good idea to do a small joint venture first, with no military technology involved, before the Americans and the Soviets tried anything on a large scale—the walk-before-you-run syndrome. I proposed a joint venture to Ambassador Dubinin, Dobrynin's successor, who sent the idea to Moscow and got a reply saying they were interested. On my next trip, I took some people who I thought would carry the idea to the next phase. We had a meeting with the Minister of Foreign Trade in a large room with a very long table. He had almost twenty people with him on his side of the table, and he proceeded to grandstand for his colleagues. I was forced to listen to the old Communist Party rhetoric about how we did them a favor by not making available our technology, which forced them to develop their own, which is always better. I was trying to be a nice guy and do something for them, but the lack of trust was so palpable that I interrupted him, saying, "Mr. Minister, you said that I have a busy schedule, and indeed I do. I see that I am already late for my next appointment." I stood up and left the room, with my bemused colleagues.

About eighteen months later, and after we had sold our interest in Bauer, Georgiy asked me to come into his office for a "four-eyes meeting," just the two of us. Making sure I was comfortable and didn't want coffee, he then, in confidential tones, suggested that we might do a joint venture making ice hockey skates in Lithuania, with the Institute as our venture partner. Everybody wants to get into the act!

———

In retrospect, it seems incredible that we could have been so worried about the USSR's ability to win the struggle with the West and dominate the world.

Yes, they had awesome nuclear weapons. But that was all. Then and now, they were a country rich in natural resources and in human talent, but poor in motivation and the skills for evolving a democracy or developing a market economy. Amongst ourselves, we often referred to the Soviet Union as a Third World country with First World nuclear capability. I have read much about the USSR, and it is clear that the people were miserably lacking in every sphere. The health care system was bad and getting worse. The educational system was not as bad, but it, too, was lapsing near the end, as the whole society disintegrated. In every social field, the Soviets were behind the West and slipping backward at an alarming rate.

I have my own theories about what went wrong under Mr. Gorbachev. First, one has to acknowledge that, toward the end of the Brezhnev era, it was obvious that the USSR was losing badly in the struggle for technological competence. And the leadership knew it, even though it was considered heretical, even treasonous, to say so.

Along came Gorbachev, the disciple of Andropov, who thought he knew the answers. He reasoned that while socialism was the right course, it had been totally corrupted by Stalin and Stalinism. If he could correct that, he would be a long way into putting socialism on the right track. Thus glasnost was invented to encourage the intellectuals to write, cinematize, and dramatize the evils of the Stalin era. Gorbachev felt it was important that the people understand that what had gone wrong was not the system, but its perversion. I wonder whether he has recognized, even now, that the system itself was fatally flawed. In a speech in Budapest in 1985, he assured one and all that socialism was the right ship. It had been badly navigated, but it was unquestionably the right ship. One notices that other aspects of freedom were not advanced—the new freedom was restricted to the criticism of Stalinism. Even Seweryn Bialer was fooled by this. Like everyone else, he reasoned that the criticism of Stalinism was but a first step. It was not. In all my travels in the USSR, I never met any Russian who understood the free-market system. Some pretended some knowledge, but on even perfunctory questioning, it became apparent that they didn't get it.

Mr. Gorbachev "invented" something new. Instead of "To each according to his need," it became "To each according to his work." He would pay people more money for more productivity. This might have worked, except for one thing—there was nothing to buy with that extra money. There was still no way to get a bigger apartment, to send one's children to a better school, to buy a suit, or shoes, or whatever. Having lived all his life in the shelter of his party perks, Mr. Gorbachev did not understand that money per se is meaningless; it is only useful in what it can buy. After about six months of working harder and receiving more useless money, under foremen who had been elected because they would make the workers produce, new elections were held and the workers elected foremen who would simply let them drink.

One problem with Russians is that they seem perfectly willing to be poor as long as their neighbors are, too. Seweryn Bialer told me this Russian story: A Russian farmer was plowing his land, and the blade struck a bottle. Out came a genie who offered him any wish in the world.

The farmer, after some thought, said OK, but that he had to explain something.

"Go ahead," said the genie.

"Well, you see this farm. It is pretty poor, and not much grass grows in my field. You see my cow, how thin it is, and how it doesn't give much milk. My chickens are skinny, and don't lay many eggs. My wife is a fat slob, and the house is always filthy, and my children are practically juvenile delinquents. Ten kilometers to the west, I have a neighbor. He has a farm the size of mine. But the soil is rich. His cow is fat and gives plenty of milk. His wife is beautiful and keeps a marvelous house, and his children do well in school and are always neat and polite."

"Yes," said the genie, "and so?"

"My wish is," said the farmer, "that you make him like me."

Alcoholism in the Soviet Union, especially in Russia, was and still is a terrible problem. The story is told that in the ancient kingdom of Kiev, Islam was rejected as the state religion because it prohibited the ingestion of beverage alcohol. Boredom and a general malaise has added enormously to this historic love of alcohol. Gorbachev's crusade against drinking led to a joke, told to me by a Russian official in Washington. It appears that an apparatchik asked his good-looking secretary to step into his office. He suggested she take off her clothes. She, in turn, suggested that perhaps she should shut the door. "Oh, no," was the answer. "They'll think we're drinking." Many Soviet citizens privately opined that the prohibition against drinking really hurt Gorbachev's relationship with the Russian people. Somehow, to most of them, getting drunk was a right, just as a job or a place to live was a right, and they felt unjustly deprived.

Gorbachev could have started his own political party early on. If he had run against the Communist Party, despite his anti-alcohol crusade, he would have won, not because he was so popular, but because the people so hated the CPSU. Then, with a real mandate, he could have told the people what had to be done to convert the command economy into a free-market economy. They might have accepted the pain. The irony is that the one man who could have done it wouldn't. As President Havel of then-Czechoslovakia said to a WJC group one evening, "There are two problems with Gorbachev. First, he does everything two weeks too late, and second, he is a Communist." That pretty well sums it up.

CHAPTER 5

GERMANY

My father had a big problem with postwar Germany, as did many Jews. He forbade me to go into business in the Federal Republic, on the grounds that American Jews would never understand Samuel Bronfman doing business with Germans.

When I argued that (a) one couldn't be in business in Europe and not be in Germany, and that (b) I was trying to take money *from* them, not give money *to* them, he remained adamant, saying, "You can go into business there when Israel and Germany exchange ambassadors." To him, that meant some few days after hell froze over. But when that event actually took place in the 1960s, I went to

Germany and bought a little liqueur company named Lehment, which operated out of Kiel. It didn't matter to me that this company wasn't big or important, I just wanted to break the ice.

I remember that visit well. Also, my quick anger if I thought a German looked at me askance. I must confess that I still have an uneasy feeling when I am in Germany. But then, since the Holocaust, Germany has had a special meaning for all Jews.

When the impoverished Federal Republic agreed to pay billions of dollars to Holocaust survivors, to Jewish organizations, and to the State of Israel, Nahum Goldmann of the World Jewish Congress was the Chairman of the Claims Conference and the chief negotiator. As Chairman, Nahum built a strong relationship with Chancellor Konrad Adenauer. Subsequently, the WJC has always had a special relationship with the Federal Republic. Indeed, we have often been criticized for being "soft" on Germans. I have found that Germans still feel guilty about the Holocaust, as they should. Despite paying billions in reparations, many feel they still "owe" Jews and Israel. So do I.

The German Democratic Republic was a different story. Early in 1990, I received a letter from Hans Modrow, then Prime Minister of the GDR, in which he, on behalf of the

East German government, at long last accepted the guilt of the Hitler era and the obligation to pay indemnities to the victims and survivors. Again, while there will never be enough money to atone for such a sin, the reparations agreement with the Federal Republic set a precedent. Since unification, the negotiations which began with the German Democratic Republic are continuing with the Federal Republic of Germany.

Also, with unification, the Federal Republic of Germany, which over the years has done a reasonable job in educating its own youth about the Holocaust, has taken on the responsibility of teaching East German youth the lessons of the Holocaust, something the German Democratic Republic had never done.

Over the years, I have met—and worked with—many German leaders, among them Helmut Schmidt and Helmut Kohl. As with other leaders, as the occasion warranted, I've criticized them and I've applauded them. I have also been quoted as saying that there is a difference between Helmuts.

Helmut Schmidt, a handsome and elegant man, who was Chancellor from 1974 until 1982, when Helmut Kohl's CDU defeated the Socialists, was a statesman and an intellectual, much like Shimon Peres. It is interesting that both are

Socialists, although "Social Democrats" might be a more appropriate term. Nahum Goldmann liked Herr Schmidt so much that he awarded him the Goldmann Medal in Amsterdam in 1980.

Schmidt was deeply wounded when Menachem Begin, to the delight of his Israeli constituency, called him a "German warrior," just as that same mouth had branded Margaret Thatcher "Brünnhilde." Politics sometimes makes even men of dignity utter unbecoming statements. On behalf of the Jewish people, I apologized to Herr Schmidt for that ugliness.

Helmut Kohl is a politician, on the other hand, which is not necessarily a derogatory term. He is extremely pragmatic, knows his constituency well, and does what he thinks necessary to ensure victory in the next election. He is also enormous—he must weigh better than 350 pounds—but he seems to have boundless energy for such a large man. I don't always agree with him, though. At a White House dinner, he sat on one side of Hillary Clinton and I sat on the other. I gave her the World Jewish Congress perspective on the Bitburg saga. Kohl had forced President Reagan to meet with him in "a spirit of reconciliation" at the gravesite of Waffen SS troops. Israel Singer had then had a good working relationship with his then-Security Adviser, Horst Telchek, and we proposed that, if they abandoned Bitburg and moved the ceremony of reconciliation to the site of Adenauer's grave, we would bring a group of important Jewish leaders. But Kohl can be stubborn, and Reagan either didn't understand the full consequences or didn't care.

Always insisting that he was "too young" to have been involved in the Holocaust, and totally rejecting the concept of collective guilt, Kohl will not accept the principle of collective responsibility. Nevertheless, a united Germany will be his greatest historical achievement. Unfortunately, his unwillingness to raise taxes to pay for that unification has brought on a terrible recession in Germany, and the rest of Europe and history may judge him harshly for this.

Which brings me to the part the World Jewish Congress played in German reunification. In 1990, when the prospect of a reunified Germany became clearly inevitable, Jews everywhere were viscerally shaken. Many still are. From many viewpoints, German aggression seems to be a historical fact: Poland always worries that Germany will expand eastward at her expense. France worries that Germany will dominate Europe, leaving her in the position of a poor relation. No doubt the British have similar misgivings.

Jews have a different perspective. We are afraid. No one should wonder at this. Our long, tragic history has touched us with paranoia, and the Holocaust was the most tragic experience of all. Out of it came the State of Israel, and Konrad Adenauer was wise enough to understand the German obligation to contribute to the building of that state. That same state must exist for all time, and must know forever that it has nothing to fear from a new, reunited Germany.

Jews believe that there must be conditions for a worldwide agreement to German reunification, and that democracy is the paramount issue. What kind of federal system emerges in a united Germany is of little importance, as long as that system is, and remains for all time, democratic. Democracy in its true form protects minorities.

When Boris Yeltsin was President of Russia (and Gorbachev was still President of the Soviet Union), I asked him to please make a strong denunciation of anti-Semitism. He was troubled, because of all the other nationalities in the country, so I asked him: "Are you not a true democrat?" The answer was an emphatic "*Da!*" I then asked if he did not agree that the essence of democracy was the protection of minorities. He agreed, and then I asked him to make a statement saying that he insisted on the protection of all minorities in the Russian Federation, including the Jewish minority. That he readily agreed to do, and a few weeks later he did.

I should think everyone would sleep easier if the world

could be assured that Germany will never be in control of nuclear weaponry, never be involved in the proliferation of nuclear weapons, and never provide the research and development for another state or group to obtain them. It is not only the Holocaust that is fresh in our minds; a poison gas factory in Libya is frightening evidence that, even of late, the Federal Republic of Germany did not have laws in its books to prevent such exports.

So when German reunification appeared to be a certainty, I asked Prime Minister Shamir the following question: "Because German reunification concerns all Jews, and because the Israeli government owes much to the Federal Republic for protection from the attitudes of the rest of the other European governments toward Israeli policies vis à vis the Palestinians, and therefore would not be able to take a position—should not the President of the World Jewish Congress make a major statement on how the Jewish people feel about it?"

The PM, after a moment's reflection, agreed. Accordingly, the WJC planned a major event with Chancellor Kohl and other notables, which took place at the lovely Jewish Center in Berlin, and at Wannsee, the place where the "Final Solution" was proposed and agreed upon. The speech I made, looking directly at the Chancellor, was well received by the audience, but it didn't exactly make Chancellor Kohl deliriously happy.

I made the following points:

1. I first reminded everyone of the fact that Berlin had been Hitler's capital, and what hell that Satan had wreaked in Europe in general, and in the death camps in particular.

2. While many Jews would not come to Berlin because of the pain it inspired, with which I fully empathized, we were there because we Jews had something to say to the new Germany. But first I reminded them that we will never forget the Holocaust, nor will they, because we will keep reminding them. And we demand an admission of collective responsibility.

3. All minorities must be protected with the full weight of the German governmental apparatus.

4. The new Germany must always have a special relationship with the State of Israel, which was born out of the ashes of the Holocaust, and must never help those who would destroy the Jewish State.

5. Germany must never be a nuclear power, or help any other state to become one. Nor may Germany ever possess chemical or germ warfare capability. I reminded them of the Libyan poison gas plant and the help German industrialists

had proffered, and insisted on strong legislation to prevent the recurrence of such an initiative.

6. The new Germany, the most powerful state in Europe, because of its aggressive history must always assure and reassure its neighbors of the sanctity of borders. And Germany must commit itself to being a part of Europe, and must help Eastern Europe maintain its democracy.

I ended by saying, "The path for the new Germany is clear. The Jewish people pray that you will prove that the world has nothing to fear; that you will follow the path away from your worst traditions and toward the best traditions of which you are so capable. The great challenge is to build a Germany firmly rooted in peace and respect for universal human values."

Many Jews in Israel, and perhaps elsewhere, refused to come to Berlin. My view is, and was, that this is a pragmatic world. I suspected then that Berlin would become the new capital of the new Germany. This, then, was the place to discuss reunification, where the symbol of its division, the infamous Berlin Wall, had come down.

To his credit, having given his approval, Shamir stuck to his guns, despite the criticism. When the press asked him about the event the day after my speech, he gave it a rave review.

What is it in the German character that made the Holocaust possible? Six million Jews and countless millions of others were put to death, not in the course of hostilities, but in cold calculation, by thousands of German citizens. If they were only obeying orders, it is even more repugnant. As a good politician, Chancellor Kohl has tried to tell the Germans that they no longer have to constantly feel guilty and less than human because of the Holocaust; that he, Helmut Kohl, has finally delivered them from this awesome burden.

Thank the Lord it hasn't worked, partly because the Jews of the world haven't let it, and partly because the Kurt Waldheim affair came at the right time.

CHAPTER 6

WALDHEIM

One cannot write about the work of the World Jewish Congress without discussing that despicable liar Kurt Waldheim, and how and why his unmasking became our responsibility.

It began in January 1986, during our Plenary session in Jerusalem. The leader of the Austrian Jewish community showed me an issue of the Viennese magazine *Profil*, which carried a report on a debate about attaching a plaque on a new air force building. The question: should it be named after a general who had been hanged as a war criminal in Yugoslavia shortly after World War II? In trying to answer in the affirmative, the article mentioned that Kurt Waldheim had served with him.

In his autobiography, Waldheim insisted that, having

been slightly wounded on the eastern front, he had returned to Vienna to continue his law studies. There had been questions from time to time about his real war record, but nothing had been found to suggest that he had done anything other than what he had said.

Intrigued, the World Jewish Congress hired a young man to delve into the records. His name was Eli Rosenbaum, and he is now Director of the Office of Special Investigations of the Department of Justice, the agency that deals with ex-Nazis. He researched Kurt Waldheim's wartime activities, and the first thing he found was that Waldheim had been a member of the "Brownshirt" storm troopers of the Nazi S.A.

His researches continued. On March 22, we released a 1948 U.S. Army document showing that after World War II, both the Army and the United Nations War Crime Commission had listed Kurt Waldheim as a suspected Nazi war criminal.

On March 25, the WJC released evidence that contrary to what Waldheim now claimed—that he was a simple interpreter—in actuality he had been a senior intelligence officer in the German army who had reported directly to the General Staff of Army Group E, with responsibility for prisoner interrogation, for testing personnel for political reliability, and, most ominously, for "special tasks," which was a euphemism for distasteful operations that could include assassinations, kidnappings, and deportations.

The next day, the U.S. Justice Department formally requested access to the documents compiled by Eli Rosenbaum for the WJC, pertaining to Waldheim.

On March 28, Senator Pete Wilson of California put a resolution on the floor, calling for the Justice Department to examine all the documents submitted by the WJC to determine what, if any, role former U.N. Secretary General Waldheim had played in Nazi war crimes.

The investigation proceeded. On April 29, the WJC released captured Nazi documents showing that Kurt Waldheim's own intelligence section had been secretly asked in April 1944 to contact the feared Nazi SS—Security Service—and German Security Police to "bring about implementation measures" for the mass deportation of nearly 2,000 Jews from the Greek island of Corfu and take them to the Auschwitz death camp.

On May 15, I was informed by our State Department that it had undertaken an investigation to determine whether Waldheim should be barred from entering the United States because of participation in Nazi acts of persecution.

On May 30, a secret file from 1948 was released by the United Nations War Crimes Commission, which disclosed a statement that Kurt Waldheim should stand trial for "murder" and "putting hostages to death."

On July 7, newly discovered documents showed for the first time that Waldheim's German intelligence unit had ordered the deportation of Greek Jews to the Auschwitz death camp. Previous documents had shown that Waldheim was the top assistant to the chief of intelligence of their headquarters section.

On July 31, to illustrate just how tight Waldheim was with his Nazi pals, we disclosed that he had been given a diary of the most sensitive secret communications and orders for the final year of the Second World War—which were all destroyed prior to their surrender. Oberleutnant Kurt Waldheim had been entrusted with this diary, according to a secret duties schedule dated February 15, 1944, which was located among captured war documents stored in the U.S. National Archives.

On November 9, 1986, the WJC released extracts from a Yugoslav dossier compiled by the Yugoslav War Crimes Commission, which stated that Waldheim was guilty of "murder" and "hostage executions." According to the secret Yugoslav criminal file, Waldheim had planned the reprisal measures of the German army in the Balkans and was responsible for the execution of hundreds of civilians. To quote from the dossier, "Based on everything herein exhibited, the State Commission declares Lieutenant Kurt Waldheim a war criminal, responsible for war crimes qualified and described above."

On April 27, 1987, Kurt Waldheim was placed on the U.S. "Watch List" and barred from entering the country, following a yearlong Justice Department investigation, which cited evidence that "Kurt Waldheim assisted or otherwise participated in the persecution of persons because of race, religion, national origin, or political opinion."

In 1988, at a press conference in Budapest, where the WJC was holding its first Governing Board meeting behind the Iron Curtain, I accused Waldheim of being "part and parcel of the Nazi killing machine." He instituted a suit against me, and to my consternation and to the delight of Seagram's lawyers, the Austrian government made him drop it. I had offers from the best lawyers the country had to offer, and I would have loved to present the evidence of his atrocious wartime behavior to the whole world.

The Austrian presidential term is for six years, and Waldheim's term ended in 1992. He wisely decided not to run again. I can report with some glee that, during his term, not one civilized country invited him for an official visit. Perhaps predictably, Chancellor Helmut Kohl greeted him on his arrival in Munich toward the end of his term. The meeting took place shortly before an election in which Kohl wanted to garner some right-wing votes.

But for those six years he was a pariah, with one exception: Pope John Paul II saw fit to invite him to the Vatican. Considering the Church's terrible record on the Holocaust, this invitation was inexplicable, and still causes a lot of pain to Jews. More recently, the Pope made Waldheim a Papal Knight. This is inexcusable, and here I should like to include the letter I sent to Cardinal Cassidy, the President of the Vatican Council that deals with the Jews, and my partner in creating better understanding between the two religions:

August 16, 1994

Dear Cardinal Cassidy,

Here in my hideaway in Sun Valley, Idaho, I read with dismay that His Holiness had seen fit to give Kurt Waldheim a papal title. That was many days ago, and I have mulled over what I should do in reaction. I thought of writing His Holiness, and then I thought that perhaps you could better convey to him my thoughts and feelings.

I cannot understand why Pope John Paul II could have done such a thing. It's like giving a rotten structure a fresh coat of paint. The structure still rots, and will still collapse. Giving such a man such an honor demeans the honor, and does nothing for the man.

Mr. A. M. Rosenthal of the New York Times was indig-

nant, and millions of people around the world must be asking the same question I am: how could the Holy Father bestow a high honor on a man who has been proven to be part and parcel of the Nazi killing machine? Anything you could do to enlighten me would be very much appreciated.

With respect and friendship,

Edgar M. Bronfman

I have never received an answer. Could that be because there isn't one that would make sense?

Some have questioned our decision to go after Waldheim. Why did we do it? Wasn't the timing bad?

We revealed the Waldheim story while he was running for President of Austria, a largely ceremonial position. In Austria, as in Germany, the President is head of state, but not head of government. He receives ambassadors, presides at state functions, and is supposedly a moral influence, as was President von Weizsacker of Germany. He made the German people conscious at all times of their past. This was not something Waldheim could honorably do, but his Nazi past had remained a secret until the WJC exposed it. Having been Secretary General of the United Nations for ten years, he seemed like a natural for the Austrian presidency. I knew we would doubtless be accused of meddling in the internal political affairs of a sovereign country, and I figured that they would probably elect him anyway. But there was a moral imperative to reveal something serious pertaining to the Holocaust. In the first round of the election, on May 4, he had slightly less than 50 percent of the vote. In the runoff election of June 8, he won with 53.9 percent of the vote. Clearly our revelations had some but not much effect.

Until very recently, Austria claimed that Beethoven was Austrian, that Hitler was German, and that Austria had been the first victim of Nazi aggression. Austria is still the head office for anti-Semitism, and Austrians are still largely unrepentant for what they did to Jews and others during the Nazi period. These were our reasons for going after Waldheim. You don't fight anti-Semitism by hoping it will go away, nor do you pretend it is less than evil. You fight it by exposing it for all its nastiness, and you expose those who would perpetrate it as racists, bigots, and xenophobes. So let it be with Waldheim.

Out of the Waldheim revelations came the opening of the United Nations files on the criminals of the Second World War. Early on, Benjamin Netanyahu, then Israeli Ambassador to the United Nations, and now Prime Minister of Israel, called to encourage me to go forward despite the criticism I was bound to get, and he continued to be a great ally throughout. We fought together for the release of the U.N. files—and won.

What was surprising was that the Jewish "street" was far ahead of the Jewish leadership. Many Jewish leaders believed this "attack" would create bad will, and worse. I believed it was a moral imperative, and everywhere I went, the audiences I spoke to were 100 percent behind me. The first such audience was at a Plenary Assembly of the Canadian Jewish Congress in Toronto, on May 8, 1986. I went into some detail in describing events as they had unfolded. The audience was on the edge of its collective seat. The roar when I finished was proof that this was a real issue for Jews.

Yes, *l'affaire* Waldheim was terrific publicity for the WJC, and put us front and center. Yes, I am proud of the role I played, and I am proud of the hard work that Israel Singer, and especially Elan Steinberg, put into the exposé. (Elan is the Executive Director of the WJC, and the executive in charge of both the North American branch and the United States section. He also directs press relations and acts as Israel Singer's right-hand man.)

But the reason I, along with Singer and Steinberg, insisted we go ahead with the campaign was that if the memory of the Holocaust were indeed fading, this would bring it back to the forefront of world attention. The criticism has since withered away, as the world has come to realize that the memory of the Holocaust must be kept alive, especially in the face of Holocaust revisionism, and that it must never be allowed to be forgotten, so that something that horrendous can never happen again.

I believe the Holocaust Memorial Museum in Washington is a wondrous thing. Shortly after it opened in 1993, my wife, Jan Aronson, and I spent four hours there. I was not only amazed at the thoroughness and good taste of everything we saw, but I was astonished at the size of the crowds who visit daily, and at the makeup of those crowds—a true cross section of Americans.

I remember a luncheon, a few years back, at the residence of then-Ambassador Richard Burt in Bonn. One of the Germans at our table criticized the Memorial Museum, which was still in its development stage, and said it would teach hundreds of thousands of Americans to hate Germans. My reply was, "This was not done by Tatars from the east, or by Martians. This was done by Germans. It is something with which you will always have to live, something we will never forget, and you are wrong, sir. Millions of Americans will visit the museum."

CHAPTER 7

EASTERN EUROPE

ROMANIA

The first time I visited Romania was in 1964, on a *Time* magazine tour of Eastern Europe. This was the second trip that Time, Inc., had organized, and it was just as fascinating as the first. I found Bucharest oppressive even then, but there was an amusing incident. The *Time* people had decided that instead of large tables at dinner, we should split up into small groups. I was seated with my good buddy John D. Harper, the Chairman and CEO of Alcoa, the Mayor of Bucharest, and an interpreter. Under such conditions, conversations are always slow, and while translations were taking place, Harper and I would exchange badinage. At one point, the Mayor asked, through the interpreter (a rather bright lady) if we didn't like each other. John indicated that I should reply, so I said, "Mr. Mayor, you don't know Americans. If two Americans are very polite to each other, it only means that they are strangers. Otherwise, they kid each other."

Having exhausted the subject of hunting, the Mayor changed tactics and said, "I'm only forty-six years old and I am a grandfather." I replied, "That's great, and what's it like going to bed with a grandmother?"

The interpreter said she would not interpret that. I said that I intended no discourtesy and would appreciate it if she left that judgment to the Mayor. I hinted that both Mr. Harper and I would feel insulted if she didn't interpret what I had said, since it was meant to be humorous. She grudgingly proceeded with the translation, and the Mayor looked somewhat bewildered, then he relaxed and said, "That must mean you like me."

The next time I visited was as President of the WJC, in 1981. I was there at the request of Chief Rabbi Rosen, the head of the Jewish community, a member of Parliament, and a man of indomitable spirit who was badly used by President Ceauşescu.

During Ceauşescu's rule, there was always a problem with

Romania and the United States' most-favored-nation treatment. According to U.S. law, MFN is dependent on human-rights behavior. Ceaușescu was not known as a Florence Nightingale, and the U.S. Congress kept him on a string by approving MFN year by year. Romania had probably gotten it in the first place because, unlike the USSR and the rest of the satellites, Romania had never broken relations with Israel after the Six-Day War.

When Ceaușescu's human-rights activities were questioned, as they were every year, the Romanian President would always send Chief Rabbi David Moses Rosen, the leader of Romania's 18,000 Jews, to the United States and to the World Jewish Congress to espouse the cause. Implicit was the threat that, if Rosen didn't succeed, there would be ugly reprisals of some kind against Romanian Jews.

Periodically, Rabbi Rosen, a man of great courage who was not lacking in self-esteem, would feel his own position threatened, and urgently pleaded with the President of the World Jewish Congress to prop him up by coming to see Ceaușescu. I did so on at least four occasions.

When I first visited Bucharest as WJC President, I was surprised at the change from the last time I had been there. Yes, there were new hotels, and the streets seemed wider and somehow more prosperous—but then I realized that the change was simply seasonal: it was summer instead of winter.

On the Saturday morning I was to see the President, Rabbi Rosen told me that all traffic would be stopped, not only automobile but pedestrian. Indeed, a good fifteen minutes before I left the hotel to walk to the palace, which took about fifteen minutes, people were stopped from walking. They just quietly stood in place. I told the functionary escorting us to hurry up, because this was embarrassing, but he told me to relax, they were used to it. We walked because it was Shabbat. I am not usually a keeper of the Sabbath, but I am when I represent the Jewish people.

Conversation with the President consisted of his mumbling into his navel, his brilliant interpreter telling Singer and me what he had said, and then his translating my part back to his boss. The conversation was mostly about MFN, and I was always successful in building up Rabbi Rosen as the great savior of Romania.

Ceauşescu served pineapple juice, which I detest, and when we returned to the hotel suite, I yelled into what I assumed was the Securitat bug that, next time, please, no pineapple juice. Either the place wasn't bugged or they ignored

my request, because the next time I came—to save two synagogues from being destroyed when Ceaușescu started level-
ing the city to rebuild it—they again served pineapple juice.
The synagogues were saved, however, and still stand. A small
price to pay.

Ceaușescu had decided to build a monument to himself.
He was going to rebuild Bucharest completely, and make it
the most beautiful city in the world. First, he destroyed cen-
turies of beautiful Romanian architecture and replaced them
with hideous modern apartment buildings—mile after mile
of sterile buildings. Then he built himself a presidential palace that would win first prize in any contest for the worst,
the biggest, the ugliest building ever built. The approaches
to this monstrosity consisted of streets lined with brand-new,
ugly offices for the *nomenklatura*. If he'd but had the time,
all Bucharest would have been destroyed.

After that first meeting, we walked to the Jewish Community Center for lunch with the American Ambassador, accompanied by a large detail of Securitat people. If anyone even
stumbled slightly in my direction, a Securitat guard would
hurl the offender against a wall or a tree. I moved into the
center of the street to avoid that kind of behavior. I have
never witnessed such dictatorial ruthlessness. Not to make a
comparison, but the only other time I've seen such hatred

in young people's eyes was when I visited Nablus on the occupied West Bank, accompanied by armed Israeli soldiers.

On another trip we landed at Constanza, on the Black Sea, near the President's summer palace at Neptune. Then came an incredible drive on a four-lane highway from the airport, with a small police car, its blue light revolving on the roof, driving in the third lane, waving all traffic away as we sped—and I mean sped—down the road, which then abruptly narrowed into two lanes. As we approached the palace guest house, the police car drove on the crown of the road, and the unlucky drivers from the other direction drove off the road and into the bushes to avoid delaying us.

The guest-house staff members asked what we wanted to eat, and we told them to give us whatever they had. Shades of Khrushchev: "Tell us what you want and we'll make it for you." Eventually, we were served passable fish, boiled potatoes, and a dessert. Some of our guys walked down the beach to a kiosk to make change so they could buy a souvenir, but were given a hard time, until a character in a suit, obviously a member of the Securitat, walked up and said something to the clerks, and then the store was theirs.

In the meantime, Singer and I went to see the Boss. What a palace! We were ushered into a room not much smaller than a football field. Singer was seated on the fifty-yard line on one side, and a Romanian flunky in uniform sat opposite him. Ceauşescu and I sat about ten feet apart, on the goal line, and in the end zone ten feet behind us sat the interpreter.

The President did his mumbling job, but the translator had no trouble. Ronald Reagan had just been elected, and I told Mr. Ceauşescu that he would be well advised to stop doing what he had been doing: that is, turning the local anti-Semites loose, and then sending Rosen to the United States to say that this would stop only if he got his precious MFN. I said his dream of a five-year MFN act of Congress was not feasible, that indeed with Reagan, a right-wing anti-Communist, in office, MFN itself was in trouble if he didn't behave.

Singer worried that we might get shot, but sometimes you have to bully a bully to get results. As a result of that conversation, anti-Semitic activity ceased for quite a while.

The last time I saw Ceauşescu, in 1988, he asked his *chef de cabinet* to get him my curriculum vitae, not something I usually carry around. I soon found out why.

Romania had now lost MFN for its inhuman-rights activities, and he had developed a new approach. When we got through with my part of the conversation, which included an account of Rabbi Rosen's good works, and I had listened to his assessment of what was happening in the Soviet Union, he said he would like to ask me some questions.

The first was, "What do you do for a living?" I explained what Seagram was. He wanted to know if there was any reason my company could not do business with his country. I replied that there was no reason I was aware of (ha!). Then he said that his First Deputy Prime Minister was waiting to discuss business opportunities with me.

I took a deep breath and told him that this wasn't how it worked. A Canadian or American company first looks at a foreign country to see what the climate is like for investment. If the political and economic climate is suitable, then we send over a team to do a feasibility study, to see if there might be a reasonable chance of success for something in our line of business. If that report is also positive, then this is the time we would meet with government officials for negotiations. I assured him that upon my return to the United States I would start the first phase of this process.

To my pleasant surprise, he smiled, nodded, and escorted me to the door, which he had never done before. While I never have, and never will, wish anyone dead, this man deserved what the Romanian people did to him. He was cruel, stupid, and so megalomaniacal that he saw himself as the world's greatest economist. He raped his country of not only its assets, but of its self-respect.

POLAND

After President Reagan had made him a pariah for impos-ing martial law in December 1981, very few people asked to see Poland's President, General Wojciech Jaruzelski. Is-rael Singer suggested to me that this might be a very good time to pay a call. We felt that the route to Soviet Jewry just might go though Eastern Europe, and it might serve us well to be gracious. I agreed, mainly because I felt that the General had probably avoided a Soviet invasion, as had happened in Czechoslovakia. So when we asked to see him, we got special treatment. Our first meeting was during his trip to New York in the autumn of 1985, when he spoke at the opening of the U.N. General Assembly session. The glasses he wore were a little off-putting, but I later learned that there was a medical reason for them. Just under six feet tall, he had a military bearing, but I detected no arrogance whatsoever.

That evening, we talked about the Soviet threat to Poland. He said he truly believed that if he hadn't taken a very firm hand in Poland in 1981, the Soviets would have marched in. I believed that he felt he was telling the truth and that he was an honorable man. He also discussed his conviction that Solidarity head Lech Wałesa was anti-Semitic. I put that in the back of my mind, and later events would convince me he was right. A few months later, I met with him again in Warsaw on my way back from a visit to Moscow. Our group stayed in the government guest house across the street from the presidential palace, and we discussed U.S./Polish relations.

It's a funny thing, but so many Europeans—and Middle Easterners, too—believe that Jewish power is quite extraordinary. Amongst ourselves, we refer to that as the Elders of Zion syndrome—the Jews are threatening to take over the world, and so anti-Semitism and pogroms are justified. He asked, "Since it's a well-known fact that the Jews control the banks and the media," why weren't we helping Poland, instead of hurting it with trade restrictions and lack of credit facilities? I went to some lengths to demonstrate that the Jews did not control the banks (I left the media part alone, because it was more difficult to demonstrate). He didn't believe me, of course, and I went on to talk about diplomatic relations between Poland and Israel. Here, I suggested that perhaps (and I stressed the word *perhaps*) the road to better relations with Washington went through Jerusalem. Not too surprisingly,

Poland started a low-level diplomatic relationship with Israel a few months later, the first so-called Iron Curtain country to do so (aside from Romania).

The last time I met with the General as President of Poland was in February of 1990, just after elections had taken place; he was still head of state but no longer head of government. This was a courtesy visit, but we did complain about an anti-Semitic incident that had just taken place, which involved a group of thugs hurling catcalls and derision at a bunch of children engaged in the March of the Living to Auschwitz. He was furious with his staff, because he hadn't been informed, and promised to do something about it. Like many of the Communist leaders I have met, the General was by no means anti-Semitic. Quite to the contrary, in the pre–World War II fight against fascism, the Communists and the Jews were often allies, and like János Kádár, he had warm memories of shared experiences with Jewish friends and neighbors.

On this same trip, we flew to Gdansk to meet with Lech Wałesa. I was not impressed with him, but under the circumstances it would have been difficult to be impressed with anyone.

There he was in his dirty office, with ashtrays dripping ashes and dead butts, wearing unpressed, ill-fitting, nondescript clothes and a filthy wrinkled tie, complaining that he was the man that had toppled communism in Eastern Europe, he was the man who had changed Poland, and (gesturing around the room) look where he was, while Havel (you could sense "that upstart") was President of Czechoslovakia. I knew then and there that he desperately wanted to be the President of Poland.

He went on to threaten American Jews in particular, and the United States generally, with disaster: if they didn't help the drowning Poles, Poland would drag us down into the sea with her (his metaphor).

I love to be threatened! In rebuttal, Singer and I said that there were millions of Americans of Polish descent who would love to help if given the opportunity. Wałesa countered by saying that he had visited America, and his impression of the Americans of Polish background wasn't very favorable. I suggested that when one is asking people for something, it is usually helpful to talk to them in their own language, and that perhaps he might consider learning English (I gather even his Polish leaves much to be desired).

And so it went. We wanted a declaration from him against anti-Semitism and, having pulled a number of teeth, we finally got it. Nonetheless, there were overt expressions of anti-Semitism later that same year during the election campaign of 1990. He charged his opponent for President, Tadeusz Mazowiecki, with being Jewish and said that those of Jewish origin "hide their nationality, they provoke anti-Semitism." He then went on to say, "I can prove my forefathers were all Poles. I am clean. I am a Pole." After the election, Wałesa disavowed that tactic, and at a meeting at the Seagram offices in New York, he told an assembly of Jewish leaders that he respected Jews and would fight anti-Semitism. The chair of the American section, Evelyn Sommer, asked him tough questions very politely, to elicit such responses.

However, you don't campaign on "Who is a real Pole," meaning not Jewish, and convince me that you are not anti-Semitic. Nor do you listen to your own favorite priest deliver an unbelievably anti-Semitic diatribe, as he did in the campaign of 1995, and later, when called upon to explain your actions, lamely suggest that you didn't hear what was being said. I wrote a letter to President Clinton, who was about to see Wałesa in San Francisco, and complained about this, and I gather the President did reprimand him.

After he was elected President, Wałesa seemed to calm down. He was no longer so insanely jealous of Václav Havel,* and

---

* Part of that jealousy no doubt arose from Poland's past. Poland has always admired, and wished to be ruled by, the elite, which means not just those with titles, but men of letters. Wałesa clearly was neither lettered nor aristocratic.

seemed to have a better understanding of the "power" of American Jews. While that so-called power is a myth, it is also true that many Americans judge the human-rights activities of other nations in terms of their treatment of their Jewish populations. During the five years of his presidency, realizing how much the prosperity of his country depended on Western help, he was mindful of both his tone and his choice of words when he spoke of Jews. He was defeated for reelection in 1995.

From Gdansk, we flew to Kraków, then drove to Auschwitz. It's hard to write about Auschwitz. It takes fierce determination. The mind and the body recoil.

First, I saw the arched sign, in German, Work Makes You Free! Then the two-story ordinary-looking brick buildings that, before World War II, had been used as barracks for the Polish army. We went inside, and as our guide told us what had taken place in those buildings, I began to reel.

Heydrich had said, First, round up the Jews and put them in ghettos: that will make it easier to carry out the rest of the plan, the Final Solution.

My tour began with photographs of insults, degradations, and ghettos. Next came Auschwitz/Birkenau itself, where Jews were divided into those who could work for a few months and those who would be put to death immediately. I saw the spot where Sophie had to make her choice, and it all became real to me.

I saw the rollers Jews had to push and pull to level the streets, and an exhibit of the hair that was cut, bulked, and sold for fifty pfennigs a kilogram, because hair was a great soundproofing agent for submarines. They also showed us a few pieces of cloth made from human hair and sold to people to wear.

I saw the shoes: prisoners were given wooden shoes, as long as there were any. Then they were given the shoes of the dead, but only if they were in bad shape. Shoes that looked reasonably good were shipped to Germany. There were children's shoes—one and a half million children were killed in the Holocaust.

I saw the personal effects: An exhibit of brushes—shaving brushes, hairbrushes, toothbrushes. Pieces of baggage with names chalked on them, to fool the victims into thinking they were going someplace other than to gas chambers and crematoria. Triple bunks piled one on top of the other, each narrow bunk "housing" two. Heaters unlit that looked like ovens. It was a warm day outside, but inside it was cold, raw, bleak, dismal.

Punishment cells: where prisoners stood four together in

a two-meter-square space all night, and if the snow blocked the air circulation, and it often did, too bad.

I gazed in horror at the wall against which prisoners were shot, and gazed numbly at the bullet holes. There were pictures of camp commander Höss with Himmler, and of Höss's house, which still stands, where he lived with his wife and four or five children. Today, they live in West Germany.

The Carmelite convent was there, too. Driving around, I saw how it dominated the site. A large cross in a field where Jews and others were made to dig their own graves. A large dog barking menacingly in the foreground. Nuns praying to convert the souls of the dead Jews to Catholicism.

Birkenau. The name means birch trees. I will never look at a birch tree the same way again. Six crematoria and underground killing rooms. Huge. Each crematorium so large that two thousand people at a time were sent to "the showers" of Zyklon B gas. It took half an hour. Then their bodies were burned in the ovens. As in a barbershop, "Next."

A survivor was there to meet with me and show me pictures—one was of his mother before she was killed. She was quite beautiful. He, a youngster at the time, survived. I wondered at something in his eyes, something near the edge of sanity. I was trying not to cry, and my anger helped.

Back in the cars to return to Kraków and the airplane, I

thought of the Bishop of Kraków, Pope John Paul II, the Carmelites, and the cross. You think about what you have seen and heard. Grown men did this to men and women and children. I couldn't speak. My mind went numb. I felt angry with myself. Somehow I should have felt more. I couldn't.

One of the problems—and traumas—the Jewish world had to face in recent times was the desecration of the site of the Auschwitz/Birkenau concentration and death camps. In 1984, a group of Carmelite nuns ensconced themselves in the building that had been used for the storage of Zyklon B. They also erected a twenty-two-foot cross, in clear violation of an international agreement, to which the Vatican was a party, that forbade any religious symbolism at the site. What's perhaps worse, the nuns were praying for the souls of those slaughtered to be converted to Christianity. A new definition of chutzpah.

On November 12, 1992, I had a private meeting with His Holiness John Paul II. At that meeting, I explained the way Jews felt about Auschwitz—that we believed that the Lord turned his face away from that terrible place, or what happened could not have happened. Therefore, any symbol of any religion was anathema. That's why Jews were so appalled at the presence of the Carmelite nuns and the giant cross.

The fiftieth anniversary of the Warsaw Ghetto uprising was due to be commemorated on April 19, 1993. I knew I wouldn't be going to Warsaw for it, because of the presence of those nuns at Auschwitz, and so I had scheduled a speech to the wine and spirits wholesalers of America in Chicago on April 20. I decided to make one last-ditch attempt to get the Pope to force the nuns to leave, however, and wrote him a letter:

March 30, 1993

His Holiness
Pope John Paul II
Vatican City

Your Holiness,

I recall with humility and pride the graciousness you extended to my colleague and myself in your study last fall.

I take the liberty of communicating directly with you, because a matter we raised at that meeting threatens the strong bonds and relations which have developed between Catholics and Jews during the course of the last several years.

Our meeting was received with overwhelming approval in the Jewish community as a sign that the many difficulties of the past were being overcome and that there was a new determination to further strengthen ecumenical ties. At a time when ethnic wars keep threatening the human condition, I shudder to think anything could harm the progress that has been made.

When we met, I indicated the appreciation within the Jewish community that the problem regarding the Carmelite convent at Auschwitz was on the way to resolution, albeit Cardinal Cassidy did express your view that the timing was a little slow. We indicated our patience.

It now appears that despite the fact of the new facilities, which were indicated at our meeting, the Carmelite nuns have refused to move, or to be removed. Jewish communities throughout the world are preparing to attend the commemoration of the fiftieth anniversary of the Ghetto Uprising in Warsaw.

Since there has been no change with respect to the evacuation of the nuns from the Auschwitz convent, the prospect of demonstrations as a result of this deplorable behavior will cause immense harm to the cause of mutual understanding, to which I believe we are both dedicated. May I therefore ask that you invoke your personal influence so that this issue can be resolved before it becomes a malignant tumor in our mutual relationship.

While I hate to write to Your Holiness on such a matter,
I am sure you understand the urgent necessity of doing so.
With greatest respect,

Edgar M. Bronfman

I don't know what it was, but on April 10, 1993, the miraculous occurred: the Pope ordered the nuns to agree to leave. As soon as we heard about the decision, I changed my plans, and instead of going to Chicago, I flew to Warsaw. The Polish government produced an outstanding program for the event. Vice President Al Gore represented the United States, Prime Minister Yitzhak Rabin represented Israel, and I represented Diaspora Jewry. President Wałesa was the first speaker, and he was dignified and solemn, just right for the occasion.

HUNGARY

The *ostpolitik* Israel Singer and I engaged in received terrific impetus from the work of one particular man, Leslie Keller, a Holocaust survivor and leader of the World Federation of Hungarian Jews.

Leslie is devoted to Jewish life and to the World Jewish Congress. When we first thought of having a WJC meeting behind the Iron Curtain, Leslie convinced us that Hungary was the place, and that he could arrange it at the highest level. Thus I was able to meet various heads of state and government in Hungary. Indeed, after the fall of communism, I was given a medal, the Order of Banners, the highest honor Hungary can bestow on a non-citizen. I cherish it because it reminds me of the ultimate victory in the USSR next door, where the Jews were finally set free—to pray, to leave, or to live with dignity as Jews.

On that first trip in May 1987, we did not meet with János Kádár, the head of the Communist Party, and the real boss. We did meet with him a few months later, in a smoke-filled room in the beautiful parliament building which had been built in the days of the Austro-Hungarian Empire. Kádár was a chain smoker—and we had hardly sat down when whiskey was served. The time was eleven A.M. This, we were told, was not unusual. On the contrary, it was customary to drink early in the day.

But the first trip was really exciting. It was during the Waldheim unmasking and it was then that I referred to Waldheim as "part and parcel of the Nazi killing machine." It got big headlines, but the essence of the meeting was not reported, and perhaps not understood, by the Western press. We were making inroads in Hungary, in terms of the ability of its 100,000 Jews to live freely and emigrate to Israel. At one critical moment, Morris Abram, then head of the Presidents' Conference as well as head of the United States Soviet Jewry movement, made his typical "Let my people go" speech, forgetting where he was. The Hungarians knew exactly where they were, and I disappeared to the washroom to discuss the crisis with our host. He wanted to stop the dinner, on the basis that one more speech like that would surely excite some retaliation from their eastern neighbor, but I managed to convince him that there would be no more similar speeches. I discussed it further with Aryeh Dulzin, the Chairman of the Executive Committee of the Jewish Agency and the World Zionist Organization, and while he made a strong speech, he did not refer to the USSR in any derogatory terms.

Like many of those old Communists, Kádár, too, said that he really liked Jews. They had been his allies in the fight against fascism in the thirties and forties. He told us stories about his old neighborhood, which had been largely Jewish—the butcher shop and the people next door. What he said was moving. It was fairly clear, however, that he was on the way out, both physically and politically. He was very sick, and his political career could not survive the waves that were tumbling Communist regimes throughout Eastern Europe.

One of the most fascinating Hungarian leaders was Harvard-trained Miklós Németh, who was Prime Minister from 1988 through 1990. I met him for the first time in May 1987, during the WJC meeting in Budapest, and he was elected a year later. In fact, he was the head of the Communist Party in the election of 1991, which of course had changed its name for political purposes, and while he won his seat by an overwhelming majority, the party lost badly, as did all the ex-Communist parties in the aftermath of the collapse of Marxism. Miklós Németh, a Renaissance man, now works in London at the International Bank for Reconstruction and Development. He is still very young, and I'm sure that someday he will return to Hungary and lead the country.

I first met the current President, Árpád Göncz, in 1990, shortly after his election, and have met with him many times since. Göncz would be perfectly cast as the benign grandfather, and could have played the lead in *Miracle on 34th Street*. His blue eyes twinkle, his white mustache twitches humorously. He is a nice human being, and a playwright. We've had long conversations about anti-Semitism in Hungary and, believe me, he has done everything he could to combat this disease. I told him, as I told Boris Yeltsin, that the true test of a democracy is its ability to protect minority groups, all minorities. That's what he must sell in his country.

I haven't seen him since 1992, when he appeared at the WJC Brussels Conference on Anti-Semitism, Racism, and Xenophobia. By then his twinkle was gone. He was worried about his countrymen and the fate of his country, especially economically. Thousands of books have been written about turning a free-market economy into a command economy, but the only one I've even heard of about reversing the process is a book by a Professor Gao in China, which I haven't as yet read. Hungary is not alone in having serious problems, of course—it's the same with all the former Communist countries. They will have to go through all the rigors of capitalism—robber barons, monopolies, excesses of every sort, antitrust legislation—until they reach the same level of development we have in the West. We can hardly learn from our own mistakes, let alone anyone else's. As the aphorism tells us, every pendulum swings too far in each direction. This will happen in these former Communist countries, too.

THE WORLD JEWISH RESTITUTION ORGANIZATION

As communism was renounced throughout Eastern Europe, a new challenge presented itself to world Jewry. All of these countries, sometimes with differing timetables, had first been occupied by the Nazis and then by the Communists. Jewish property had been stolen by the Germans and then by their successors. Now was the time to demand justice.

There are differing definitions of property. There is private property—homes, jewelry, etc.—which heirs wanted returned; there is heirless property, because the heirs were slaughtered; then there is communal property—synagogues, community centers, schools, hospitals, and the like. In 1992, the World Jewish Restitution Organization was established, consisting of such Jewish organizations as the Holocaust Survivors, the Jewish Agency, B'nai B'rith International, the Joint Distribution Agency, and, of course, the State of Israel. I was asked to head it, probably because of my solid reputation in Eastern Europe. In that guise, I also represented the Israeli government; there is a signed agreement between Minister of Finance Shochat and me to that effect. Our brief was to negotiate for the return of heirless and communal property. We were also to help any heirs who applied to find the correct avenues for the recovery of private property.

Many countries might claim that heirless property automatically reverts to the state. In those cases, we ask each country to pass legislation to return the property to the WJRO, on behalf of the local community and the Jewish people.

Much property is also being returned in what was East Germany, and that is administered by the Conference on Jewish Material Claims Against Germany, the group once headed by Nahum Goldmann and now under the watchful eye of Rabbi Israel Miller. I have been asked to play a role in that organization as well.

The two men most responsible for pushing forward the work of the WJRO are Israel Singer of the WJC and Zvi Barak of the Jewish Agency. Naphtali Lavie, also of the Agency, does yeoman work as well. In our efforts, we have managed to get the cooperation of both the Congress of the United States and the European Parliament. In April 1995, Singer, Barak, and Elan Steinberg went to Washington to visit Senators Dole, McConnell, and Helms, and Representatives Gilman, Gingrich, and Gephardt. Out of it, we received a letter expressing congressional support for the efforts of the WJRO, which has been very useful in convincing the regimes in Eastern Europe that they should cooperate.

In early September 1995, we visited Brussels and urged the European Parliament to be similarly supportive. This effort was even more important, because the Eastern European countries see their economic future as members of the European Community. The upshot was that in December

1995, key legislation was enacted by the European Parliament.

I really don't know how much money we're talking about. It could be billions, especially if one includes properties in East Germany. But there are real problems. We are dealing with countries without much money. We are dealing with Jewish communities—the remnants that survived World War II—and the Communist regimes that followed are sometimes inclined to think that the monies belong to them, and not to Israel and the Jewish people. We have attempted to solve both those problems by being patient on the question of cash, asking only that the claims be acknowledged and verified; with the local communities, we have set up charitable trusts, with the WJRO holding the majority position, but including representation from the local community as well. In Hungary, where there is a sizable Jewish community of some 100,000, the Hungarian government is about to pass the enabling legislation, and the charitable trust has been set up.

Poland is a real headache for us, and more certainly for them. There were some 3.3 million Jews there before 1939. There are perhaps 5,000 left. The amounts of communal properties that serviced a population like that is mindboggling. Now that Lech Wałesa is no longer President, we may make some headway, but this is going to be a long hard struggle.

Slovakia has been very forthcoming, as has Bulgaria, the only country in the region that did not surrender its Jewish population to the Nazis. Romania has passed the enabling legislation. It gets a little more difficult as one crosses the frontier of what was the Soviet Union. I'm referring particularly to properties stolen by the Nazis and subsequently by the Communists in Lithuania, Latvia, and Estonia. But with the leverage of the United States and the European Community, we hope we shall prevail.

Another potentially huge issue is the monies held in safe-deposit boxes in Swiss banks — not just the monies that had been deposited by Jews, but the monies that had been stolen from Jews by Nazis and then deposited in Swiss banks. After we left Brussels in September 1995, we went to call on the Swiss Bankers Association. First we met with Swiss President Kaspar Villager. I thought at first that the meeting was merely a matter of form, but I later learned that the Swiss government was vitally concerned with the whole issue, and now we have more meetings with government officials set up.

Then we went to our lunch with the Swiss Bankers Association, which was scheduled for twelve-thirty at a private club. We got there first and waited while they caucused. When they came out, Dr. George Krayer, the President of the SBA, but not a major player, said that before we went into lunch—we were in an anteroom—he would like to read a statement. The tactic, which was very fresh and seemed to be the reason for the caucus, was to get our side to agree that the $30 million-odd that they proposed to give over to the WJRO was all there was, and there wasn't any more. The idea that there was much more money to be had, he continued, was ridiculous, and in their great generosity they had set up an ombudsman, and as part of that office they had asked Leon Schlumph, a former President of Switzerland and now head of a major charitable organization, to help those with claims. When he ended his written speech, he asked me to respond.

Clearly, I was supposed to be impressed with their generosity and their goodwill, and equally clearly I was supposed to accept the money, and then we could all go and have a pleasant lunch. I guess I disappointed them. I started out by saying that we really hadn't come to discuss money, but to discuss procedure. I told them that I was a businessman but not a banker, and that I would have to consult with banking friends, such as Felix Rohatyn, James Wolfensohn and Seagram's regular bankers, Goldman, Sachs and Company. They seemed somewhat shocked at my answer, but nonetheless we went into the next room for lunch. We were on the side of the table facing the light, and my place card had my surname spelled with not two but three *n*'s.

Krayer did most of the talking for their side, as did I for ours. We heard a lecture about the size of the Swiss banks in the thirties, how ridiculous it was to think that huge amounts could have been deposited in those days, and further assertions that they were acting in good faith and were to be trusted. "We don't want one franc which doesn't belong to us," said Krayer, the one thing he did say with which we could agree. I quoted Ronald Reagan in his meetings with Mikhail Gorbachev: "Trust, but verify." Israel Singer showed a letter from Prime Minister Rabin that authorized me to act on behalf of the Israeli government, which seemed to impress them.

Finally, the atmosphere relaxed a little, and I explained to them our position. If they expected the WJRO to tell the whole world in general, and the Jewish world in particular, that what we were now hearing was indeed the truth, then we would have to be involved in the procedure. Krayer proposed a committee made up of people from each side to monitor that procedure, and I agreed in principle. A little while later, we left, to face a barrage of press.

We have a long way to go, but in one of our meetings to help pry loose information, Senator Alfonse D'Amato of

New York, Chairman of the Senate Banking Committee, actually rubbed his hands with glee when we proposed that he become active in this effort. He will be of enormous help. He may even be able to get the OSS files for us, which will disclose much information as to exactly what transpired in the immediate aftermath of the Second World War.

CHAPTER 8

LATIN AMERICA

My first trip to South America was in the spring of 1969. Ann and I went in the *Seagram Gulfstream II* with our very close friends, Bill and Judy Green, and we covered Venezuela, Chile, Argentina, and Brazil. I went because I wanted to see a region of the world where Seagram was about to become important. We found much that could be admired and much that couldn't, but during the entire length of the visit I never asked about Jews. That was to come later.

When I first attended a World Jewish Congress meeting under Nahum's gavel, I noticed that as soon as anyone spoke Spanish, some people rudely got up and left the room, newspapers rattled, and the noise level noticeably increased. At first, I thought it was the language itself, but it soon became apparent that most Jews throughout the Diaspora and from Israel had little interest in what transpired in Latin America.

Israel Singer and I decided that, under my presidency, it would be different. When we first began to travel to South America, almost every country was a dictatorship, with the possible exception of Venezuela, which might have been characterized as an oligarchy. Until very recently, Mexico has toyed with some democratic trappings, but trappings is the word for it. In its system, a man is "elected" president for a six-year term by being appointed the candidate of the ruling party, the PRI, by his predecessor, and in turn appointing his successor. In the process, if he plays his cards right, he manages to steal hundreds of millions of dollars.

The only one of those guys I ever really "admired" was Miguel Alemán. He found a unique way to use the power of the presidency. Recognizing the enormous future of Acapulco as a premier resort area, he simply bought all the land along the coast east of the town, and then moved the airport, which was in a lousy and inadequate area anyway, just to the east of his holdings. As hotels began to spring up, they were, for the most part, built on his lands, and of course the price of that real estate multiplied geometrically.

Shortly after my first election, in 1981, we took a trip to

São Paulo, where the Latin American Jewish Congress was holding its annual meeting. São Paulo is an ugly city, with little to recommend it to the tourist. It is the largest city in the Americas, with resultant horrible traffic jams and pollution. The Jewish community of Brazil is about 150,000 souls, with some 50,000 to 60,000 in Rio de Janeiro, a similar population in São Paulo, and the rest scattered in the larger cities to the south. São Paulo has a large Jewish community center, and we went to meetings there every day for three days.

As the newly elected President of the WJC, I was expected to say a few words, and I did. My speech was basically in favor of democracy and against dictatorship, for Jewish survival—which is best guaranteed in democracies—and with support of Israel thrown in. The head of the Latin American Jewish Congress was an Argentinian, as was the practice, since the largest number of Latin American Jews were Argentinian, some 250,000 to 300,000. After my speech, which I thought was well received by most, I received a summons to appear before the Argentine delegation, and given a lecture on the politics of living under a dictatorship, as they did, as opposed to having an American passport, as I did. I answered by saying that it was the duty of the large and powerful Jewish communities to protect the smaller ones, and that just because I would return to New York after the meeting did not mean that I would forget them, and that should trouble come their way, I would be the first to protest loudly in the United States and in Argentina. That satisfied them somewhat, but it certainly would have been an embarrassment to them if I had given my speech in Argentina proper. I had so much to learn!

I have tried to make a trip to South America every two years since then. We have a great friend in São Paulo, Henrique Rosset, who holds a dinner and fund-raiser for the WJC each time we visit his community, and through his efforts, the Latin American Jewish Congress is practically self-sufficient financially. Because the largest percentage of Latin American Jews live in Argentina, that's where we and the Latin American Jewish Congress have our administrative offices, overseen by Professor Manuel Tennenbaum, a talented teacher and a great executive.

As of now, South America is democratic, from Tierra del Fuego to Belém, from Antofagasta to Rio de Janeiro. I have visited most countries there, and some of the newly democratically elected presidents have visited with us in New York. President Collor of Brazil was one of them.

When Collor was first elected in December 1989, there was a great deal of hope and expectations. Brazil had finally shaken off the army and, for the first time in many years, had elected a civilian President. I first met President Collor in New York a month after he was elected, on January 25, 1990. It was his way of saying that he respected the Jewish people. I met him again in August 1990 in Brasilia, that noble experiment that has become a rather shabby city in Brazil's interior. The jungle has crept back, slowly having its way. The evening before our meeting with the President, the Israeli Ambassador held a dinner in his home and proudly showed me a brand competitive to Chivas Regal, as if he were doing me a favor. He learned.

My first impression of President Collor was of a very handsome, tall, rather Teutonic-looking man, who made everyone feel immediately at ease, even in the unfamiliarity of New York's Waldorf Astoria Hotel. This was much more pronounced when we met on his turf in Brasilia. Our Seagram executive in charge of South America, whose office was in São Paulo and who was with us, also got royal treatment. I discussed U.N. Resolution 3379, which equated Zionism with racism, and Mr. Collor offered to be a sponsor of the necessary resolution to vacate it.

Democracy in Brazil has survived the Collor scandals, and President Cardoso, a brilliant economist who oversaw Brazil's economy as Finance Minister, is making the democracy stronger month by month. I have visited with him in my apartment in New York, and in Brasilia, and I am continually impressed.

There are some 25,000 Jews in Venezuela, mostly in Caracas. They enjoy a great school, in fact so good that many non-Jews attend, but still, after high school, the Jewish students go to university and meet and often marry non-Jews. The pattern of assimilation that we see in North America is more applicable to Venezuela than it is to the other communities of Latin America, including Mexico. Nevertheless, they have a good community. One of the interesting things I learned there is that most of the country's rabbis come from the United States, as do those of São Paulo and Buenos Aires. Here I must pay tribute to Pinchas Brenner (known as Pinky to his friends) of Caracas, and Henry Sobel of São Paulo.

The Jews of Argentina are, by and large, middle or lower middle class. The country by definition is "the Catholic Republic of Argentina," and anti-Semitism also seems to be written into the country's name. With all the persecution they received at the hands of the military dictatorship, I have sometimes wondered why many more Jews have not made *aliyah* and gone to Israel. The answer is that they live very well, as help is cheap and they have a country-club life in a very temperate climate, which is pleasing. Their standard of living would be greatly reduced should they leave. Of course, the overt persecution stopped with the change to democracy, but I am told that anti-Semitism is still rampant.

The Falkland Islands war finished the Argentinian military dictatorship. Their defeat at the hands of the British was devastating to the entire populace, causing a fervent anti-military feeling. As a result, Raúl Alfonsín was elected President on October 30, 1983. Not long after that, I met him for dinner with a small group in his presidential mansion. I soon found out why we were getting special treatment. The President asked me to take a message to Margaret Thatcher: If it were important to her that democracy become firmly entrenched in Argentina, she could help enormously by giving back the Malvinas (their term for the Falkland Islands) and then take a lease—for as long as she wanted. To emphasize his point, he asked me to tell the British Prime Minister that he was willing to swim all the way to England to accomplish this goal.

I did speak with Mrs. T. about his proposition, and her answer was, "Sovereignty, sir, it's a matter of sovereignty, and we shall never give that up. Tell Mr. Alfonsín to swim back to Argentina." Lord Lever, a friend as well as a Jew, and proud of it, said that when a new (meaning Labour) government came in, it would be possible to discuss it with some degree of rationality, but not until then. As of this writing, that still hasn't happened.

When President Carlos Saúl Menem was elected to succeed Alfonsín in Argentina, the country was in a real mess, and Alfonsín turned over the reins of government earlier than the constitution provided. Menem had been scheduled to take power on December 10, 1989, but he actually took over on July 9. The local Jews were somewhat panicked. Menem had run as a Peronista, and the memories of that rule were unpleasant, to say the least. In addition, Menem was a Syrian, and people were worried that he would really stick it to the Jews and to Israel. Imagine our surprise when he decided that the first official foreign visitor he would meet would be me. It was on July 31, 1989, very soon after his installation, and it was a most enjoyable meeting. He looked like a successful hippie musician, with his long hair and his Hollywood attire, but once he started speaking, I knew I was in the presence of a very shrewd man. As I got to know him better, I also realized that he was a very nice, warm, and charismatic human being.

On another occasion, as we sat down, I said the following: "Mr. President, if the Argentine people aren't wise enough to give you what you ask [he wanted a constitutional change to make the presidential term limit two consecutive—and elected—four-year terms instead of one six-year term], there's a country to the north that is in need of an honest and capable President. I think I might be able to arrange that if, of course, you bring Cavallo with you." Ernesto Cavallo was the brilliant Minister of Finance who has done so much to make Argentina's financial comeback possible. On that same visit, the Foreign Minister announced to us in his office that, despite the fact that the ruling party was known as the Peronistas, they were prepared to open the archives and let the world examine the records of the aftermath of World War II, with particular respect to Nazis who had sought refuge in Argentina. I'm particularly anxious to find out what the Roman Catholic Church under Pope Pius XII did in this regard, to aid and abet fleeing war criminals.

The Argentinian Jewish community has been greatly shaken by two terrorist bombings in the last few years. Terrorism is one of the ugliest manifestations of the diseased mind at the end of this century. The first was on March 24, 1992, which destroyed the Israeli embassy and took many lives, and the second on July 18, 1994, which destroyed the Jewish community center building and took one hundred lives. I visited the country after each incident.

On my trip after the embassy was bombed, I spent time with the Israeli Ambassador, who carefully surmised that the bombing was perhaps a direct result of the very good relationship that now existed between Argentina and Israel, especially in comparison with previous regimes. Somehow, though, the bombing of the embassy was not nearly so devastating to the Jews of Argentina as was the destruction of their community center two years later. Perhaps it was because this second bombing was directed not at Israel or the peace process, but at the Jews of Argentina, in a very personal and savage way.

I spent a momentous twenty-four hours there, on July 27 and 28, trying to help the community rebuild itself out of the literal ashes of the community center.

Jan and I had been visiting our good friends Leah and Israel Klabin in their wild but beautiful home on the Mato Grosso in western Brazil. On learning of the bombing, and being told it was all right to visit, I called Israel Singer, who then flew by commercial airplane from New York to Rio de Janeiro, with Jan's and my hanging bags on his shoulder, where the Seagram plane picked him up and flew him to Campo Grande, where we boarded and went to Buenos Aires.

On the way in from the airport, we called at the Sholem Aleichem school, a Jewish educational institute in a poor neighborhood—as I've noted, the Jews of Argentina are not wealthy—that goes from pre-kindergarten through high school. We went into a first-grade classroom, and the kids were marvelous, then we went into the main auditorium, where the entire student body was in place, awaiting us. After an overlong speech by the school director, I spoke a few words, and asked them all to say with me *"Am Yisrael chai"* — the Jewish people live. And because we thought that the terrorist attack was inspired by the success of the peace process in the Middle East, I also asked them to repeat *"Am Yisrael chai bishalom"* — the Jewish people live in peace.

Then it was their turn. They sang and recited works they had created, the essence of them being, "We shall atone, we shall console, and then we shall go on, proud of our tradition." I was teary-eyed by the time they were through. I have seldom been so moved!

Then we met with the Foreign Minister, Guido di Tella. He told us of his family background, of people who had fought fascism forever, and that while it was most unusual for a Latino foreign minister to apologize for anything, he was apologizing for what his country had done, in terms of being a refuge for Nazi war criminals, and for his country's anti-Semitism. With a gesture, he said, "Mengele practiced medicine here for ten years. . . ."

That evening we met with President Menem. He, too, was devastated, and it was obvious that he took the attack personally. Our delegation consisted of Jan; Reuben Baraja, the head of the local Jewish community; Israel Singer; Manuel

Tennenbaum; Benno Milnitsky, President of the Latin American Jewish Congress; and me. I pointed out to President Menem that the perpetrators of the embassy bombing two years before were still at large, and asked him to do everything possible and more to apprehend the bombers of the community center. He vowed that they would be caught. As of this writing, however, they are still at large! And the trail is very cold. Could it be that the security and intelligence services of Argentina are not particularly good? Or that the country's long history of anti-Semitic and anti-Israel behavior have led them to be not particularly efficient, despite the urgings and admonitions of their President? In any case, I suggested that it would be a great example of his good faith, and a much-needed indication of his solidarity with the community, if he should see his way to announce the government's intention of rebuilding the community center. This he agreed to do.

From the Casa Rosada, the Argentinian equivalent of the White House, we went to a temporary Jewish headquarters building for a meeting of all the presidents of the Jewish communities throughout Argentina. The next morning, we met with some press, and then with Argentine Jewish leaders to make some plans to raise money outside of Argentina to help put the community back on its feet. And then we called on the Israeli Ambassador. He was exhausted and asked to speak in Hebrew because he was too tired to speak any other language. Israel Singer translated that the Ambassador was concerned about the fact that Reuben Baraja was going to testify to the U.S. Congress, and what effect that would have on the Argentine government, while he assured us that never had relations been so good between Israel and his host country. Both Singer and I assured him that Mr. Baraja was very sensitive to the situation.

At the luncheon that Reuben Baraja gave at his bank, I told all the leaders of the Jewish community in Argentina that I wept with them, that I grieved with them, and now I would rebuild with them, for life must go on, and the community would look to its leaders for guidance, and we all had to face up to the task. I urged them to make every effort to reopen those community activities that had been shut out of fear, and to remember that they were not alone, that the entire Jewish world was there with them. That was the import of my being there—to tell them that world Jewry was there with them, expressing its solidarity at a time of crisis.

In fact, that very day, the Chair of the American section of the WJC, Evelyn Sommer, who had been born and raised in Argentina, had held an enormous rally in New York to mourn the dead, and to express solidarity with the Argentine community.

Before I went to the airport, I visited a victim of the bombing named Mrs. Neff, who was in the hospital with her husband and son. She had heard the awful news of the death of another son in that same blast. There were deep cuts on her face, her mouth was twisted as if she had had a stroke, and I gather she was paralyzed. What can you say to such a person? Thankfully, the hospital didn't let us stay for more than a couple of minutes. I'm told she was glad that we had come, but tragedies like that are only news items until you meet the victims. Then they become overpowering. I will never forget the terrible things that I saw that day. I pray to Hashem that I shall never have to see their like again.

CHAPTER 9

ISRAEL

Israel has played a role in the life of every Jew extant, big or little, but a role—and it has played a very large part in the lives of the Bronfmans.

My first trip to Israel was in 1956. Our father's sixtieth birthday had been celebrated in 1951, and Minda, Phyllis, Charles and I had endowed the Israel Museum with the money to establish the Samuel Bronfman Archaeological and Biblical Museum. The structure was now ready to be dedicated, along with the museum's new Billy Rose Garden and the building containing the Dead Sea Scrolls, and we all flew to Israel for the ceremonies.

Jerusalem was still divided at the time, and the hotel was

fairly close to the border between Israel and Jordan. Standing at the windows of the King David Hotel, I could see the Jordanian soldiers standing guard on buildings nearby. They seemed menacing, and it quickly brought home to me the stressful circumstances of Israeli life. They were a nation surrounded by their enemies, in a constant state of war, forced to live with a siege mentality. I had sometimes described the average Israeli as rude, and mentally I asked forgiveness. If you're always afraid that tomorrow might bring another war, you're entitled to be less than polite, especially to American Jews, with their air of superiority.

Ann was pregnant at the time with Holly, our third child. When we arrived, Father said that Ben-Gurion, who knew of her condition, had asked if this child could be dedicated to Israel. Ben-Gurion never really understood why American Jews stayed in America. He had never been there, and he wrongly assumed that the United States was just another country in the Diaspora, and, like the other countries of his experience, one in which it was a great disadvantage to be Jewish. I don't think he appreciated the fact that American Jewry had found their Zion. He had at first been shocked, and then disdainful, that American Jews hadn't flocked to Israel after the state had been established. There is a certain amount of that attitude, generally in Israel, for the Diaspora. Some of it is based on the assumption that, with rates of assimilation ever rising, the Diaspora is doomed.

In 1948, when Israel won its independence, I was too young really to appreciate what the Hagana had accomplished with such bravery and perseverance. I well remember the 1956 war, however, which came in November, some eight months after my visit to Jerusalem. The Egyptians had seized the Suez Canal, and the British and French were at first very hesitant to act. Harold Macmillan was Prime Minister of England, and wasn't what one might call Churchillian. The French were, as always, French. The Israelis were the only ones to act, and finally their so-called allies gave in to American pressure and agreed to support them.

The whole thing was unfortunate. By the time the French and the British finally agreed, it was almost election day in the United States. You don't present an American President with such an aggressive plan on the eve of his reelection. Either the whole operation should have been successfully concluded, or it should have waited until after the election. I was not critical of Eisenhower so much as I was of the French and the English, who were lacking either in the courage of their convictions or in their courage, period.

However, like everyone else, both Jewish and not Jewish, I really was excited and ennobled by the Six-Day War in

1967. That event was a defining moment in Jewish history—suddenly, the vast preponderance of world Jewry was
proud to be Jewish. A new joke made the rounds: one child
complains to his mother that he is playing Jew and Arab with
his friend—who won't let him be a Jew. The rest of the world
was suddenly more respectful of Israel, even in such unlikely
places as Texas, where they still didn't like American Jews very
much, but they sure admired Israelis.

———

Golda Meir was Prime Minister of Israel the second time I
visited the country, in the fall of 1972, more than a year after
Father's death. Ann and I were in the process of separating
by then, and so I traveled with my good friends Bill and Judy
Green.

First we visited the Weizmann Institute, where we met
Meyer Weisgal, a man with a sensational sense of humor, who
was known as Israel's number one fund-raiser. We visited all
the "must-see" places, such as Masada, the Dead Sea, Herod's
Palace, and Yad va-Shem, and even ate a meal with a nomadic
Bedouin family. It was a strange feeling, since we were in occupied territory and we had no idea how welcome we really
were. An army officer named Yitzhak Segev accompanied us
with two soldiers, and when we asked if he was having any

trouble with the native population, he slowed the Jeep to a spot where some Arabs were digging, and pointed out how much money they were getting for quarrying Jerusalem, as compared to what they had gotten before the Six-Day War and Israeli occupation. That seemed to say it all—at least for him. Later events were to prove otherwise.

We managed to spend one evening in Tel Aviv at the home of Shimon Peres and his wife, Sonya, and their daughter. I was very impressed with this man who later turned out to be such a close friend to so many Bronfmans. We also visited Caesarea, Sfad, and a kibbutz on the shore of Lake Galilee, and were dutifully impressed with the bravery and hard work of the members, but I remember feeling that I wouldn't want my children taken away and brought up by others, even in the same community. We also got a talk about the Golan Heights, and how snipers had made their lives so dangerous and difficult before the 1967 war. This is important to re-member now, as Israel contemplates a return of these stra-tegic heights to Syria. It's hard, when you have been told for almost thirty years that a certain piece of land is necessary for your security, to be assured. "Well, maybe it's not that vital."

We did have coffee with Golda in her kitchen, as everyone seemed to do when visiting her, and I remembered how my father had bristled at her intractable attitude toward the Palestinians, who, she had been fond of saying, did not exist. But I did not make a point of it, and we had a reasonably relaxed time. I was still not committed to Judaism or all that involved with Israel. My feelings were that I would be crushed if anything happened to make the Jewish State disappear, but that I didn't feel much of a personal responsibility to make sure it didn't happen.

————

My next trip to the Holy Land was in 1974, on another *Time* tour. I had traveled to London on Seagram business first, and then caught up with Jim Linen, the President of Time, Inc., at Gatwick. From there, I flew on their G-2 with him to Cairo to meet with the rest of the group. We always saw heads of state and government on those trips, and this one was no exception. None of the sessions was that remarkable, except for the willingness of the Arab heads to see us, to answer questions, and try to put their best foot forward. I'm sure they thought we had enormous influence in the United States. From Cairo we went to Beirut, Lebanon, a lovely city at that time, where we met government officials and had dinner in a mountain retreat. At that time, Saudi princes kept chalets in those Lebanese mountains, where it was relatively cool.

From Beirut, we traveled to Damascus. Arafat was scheduled to meet with us there, and the very few Jews who were on our trip had to determine whether or not they would see him or, perhaps more important, be *seen* with him. I had no doubts. I wouldn't have met with him one on one, but with that large group, I felt perfectly comfortable. It all came to naught, however, as he didn't appear—called off to some other emergency, we were told.

Amman, Jordan, came next, where we first met Crown Prince Hassan, who delivered a lecture on the growing economy and his plans for the future, and then had the honor of meeting King Hussein. The aircraft stayed in Amman and we bused across the Allenby Bridge into Israel. As we traversed that tiny span, I grabbed the microphone and said, "*Goyim* to the back of the bus."

The Israelis, never very good at *hasbara,* or propaganda, took us to the battlefield where General Raphael Eitan had defeated the Syrians in 1967, and then to an air force base, where the Israelis demonstrated how fast they could refuel and rearm their aircraft, which made the enemy think they had at least twice as many planes as they did. That was all well and good, but I was not impressed with the show they put on, and even less so when we went to Jerusalem. Rather than trying to prove they were the toughest kid on the block,

I believed that they should have shown the cultural and humanitarian side of Israel to our group. They claimed that they were showing Americans to what good use they were putting the weaponry America provided, but I didn't think that was appropriate. They didn't even insist that the group visit Yad va-Shem and pay their respects to the 6 million murdered in the period of the Holocaust. I spoke to Teddy Kollek, the charming Mayor of Jerusalem, about this, and he shrugged his helplessness.

A few years later, I got to have my say, though. Another *Time* tour to Israel was in the works, and this time Phil Beekman, the Seagram COO, was going. I huddled with Yossi Ciechanover, my friend and an official of the Israeli Foreign Office, and proposed that Israel see to it that the group saw not only Yad va-Shem, but the Hadassah Hospital, the Israel Museum, and the Old City. He pointed out that Time, Inc., was concerned only with meeting top Israelis. "Fine," I said. "The minister of whatever will meet the group at the administrative offices of whatever. Just insist, and they will see what you want them to see." It must have worked, because when the group returned to New York, I got a call from Jim Linen, saying he had seen my fine Italian hand at work.

From Jerusalem, we bused back to the Amman airport

and flew to Kuwait. I was curious about how I had been issued a visa to this country, which was not friendly to Jews,
and was told that the Saudis had arranged it. The most curious thing about Kuwait to me was the fact that the Palestinians resident there did all the work that demanded
bright people—but they weren't allowed citizenship. To get
that, a person had to demonstrate Kuwaiti grandparents on
both sides. Small wonder, I suppose. Thanks to the country's
oil revenues, Kuwaiti citizens received lots of benefits—free
education, no taxes, plentiful water from expensive distilla-
tion plants, and the like. We met with the Emir—a very
unimpressive audience. The first night we were there there
was no beverage alcohol—they were the hosts. The second
night the Kuwaitis made up for what they had missed the
first night—there was plenty of alcohol, as Time, Inc., was
the host.

Abu Dhabi was next, where the Hilton was brand-new and
the service impeccable. Again we met with dignitaries, but
again the meetings were perfunctory and we learned nothing
new. After a side trip to Dubai, it was on to Saudi Arabia. The
Saudis took the prohibition against drinking beverage alcohol seriously, and we were given bunches of miniatures just
before we deplaned in Riyadh. When asked what we should
do if any official asked pertinent questions about it, we were

told to deny everything, and refuse to put up with the indignity of a body search.

When we got to our rooms, some of us were disturbed by the hotel operator, who was trying to connect us to telephone calls placed days earlier by a previous guest! A most unusual thing occurred, as well. Our hosts, the Saudi royal family, provided each of us with a Samsonite briefcase containing a copy of that infamous forgery *The Protocols of the Elders of Zion*, in English. We never did figure out why they thought that was appropriate!

They also invited our group to attend an execution in the town square, which some people actually went to (*not* yours truly, however). Most of us went to a much tamer meeting with the American Ambassador, who was clearly an Arab sympathizer. We all met with then-King Faisal and Crown Prince Fahd, who is the current King. We were allowed to ask questions, and what we heard about the prospects for peace was not very illuminating. I was since told that the Saudis paid off everyone in the Arab world to leave them alone, including the Palestinians. They were also well known for not ever saying yes, in terms of the peace process, but always being enigmatic.

That about ended the trip, except for a brief stop in Rabat, Morocco, where we were gathered together to try to come to some conclusions as to what we had seen and heard. My own conclusion was simple: even though they were reasonably polite about it, the Arabs were implacable about the opposition to a permanent Jewish State in what they considered Arab territory. It would take a miracle to get them to change their minds.

———

No miracles were in sight on another trip to Israel in 1976, but we were treated to a seder, my favorite Jewish ceremony, at Sharm el Sheikh. Our host was then–Minister of Defense Shimon Peres, and we flew there from Jerusalem in a Hercules transport plane with President Ephraim Katzir. The seder itself took place in the mess hall of the naval forces.

After a very lengthy service by Chief Chaplain Goren of the IDF, who was about to retire, we watched the young people dance the hora on the ships in the docks. The next day, Shimon invited me to a meeting with him just north of Tel Aviv. He apologized for the length of the service, although no apology was needed, and commented that being a rabbi was no job for a nice Jewish boy. Okay—but I hadn't heard it before.

Yitzhak Rabin was the Prime Minister, and I did meet him on several occasions in his home and at his Knesset office.

My first impressions were of a rather cold man, not particularly well versed in economic matters, with a deep, cigarette voice. It's amazing how those first impressions changed over the years! Rabin was forced out of office due to some minor scandals and the fact that a flight of F-15s had landed in Israel on the Sabbath. More's the pity, because in the election that ensued, Menachem Begin became Prime Minister Begin: Ben-Gurion's forever enemy, the disciple of Vladimir Jabotinsky, the hard-liner who neither wanted to accept German reparations money nor agreed that Israel should have accepted the United Nations' partition line of 1947.

I had an up-and-down relationship with Begin. On the one hand, whenever he took actions that I felt imperiled peace, I said so, vocally, and sometimes on the op-ed pages of the *New York Times*. On the other hand, he *was* the Prime Minister now, and it was important that we work together.

I asked pollster Lou Harris to do a study on why Mr. Begin had won the election, and on the Prime Minister's first trip to New York, Lou and I went to his Waldorf suite to examine the results. Lou pointed out that the basic difference between this and previous elections was that this time the Moroccan Jews had solidly backed Likud, Mr. Begin's political party. Begin was intrigued, and this began a long relationship.

I have always wanted peace for Israel, not at any cost, but

an honorable peace that would allow Israel to live in security with its neighbors. Of course, there was, and will be, disagreement about what constitutes defensible borders. I got to know President Carter's National Security Advisor, Zbigniew Brzezinski, quite well, and in one meeting, knowing that I and many like-minded friends were very much against Begin's settlements policy, he asked me why we couldn't affect the Israeli government's construction of settlements across the Green Line, the old borders of Israel, pre–Six-Day War. I asked if he meant because of the large gifts we donated. He said that is what he meant, and I told him that the entire Jewish world gives Israel some $600 million a year, and the United States government gave over $2 billion. "If you can't affect Prime Minister Begin's policies, how do you expect us to?" But the truth of the matter is that neither I nor any of my friends would ever use our gift dollars to Israel as leverage to affect the security of the state, which, Begin claimed, was the purpose of the settlements.

The Prime Minister was always courtly and respectful to me. I was told that he didn't really like wealthy people, but our problems were based on ideology, and not wealth. On the other hand, I was told about one occasion when he went to the Jerusalem airport, Aharot, to fly to Alexandria for a meeting with Sadat. He saw a large (comparatively speaking) jet aircraft looming over the Westwind that he was about to enter. He asked about the bigger plane and, when told it belonged to Seagram, he grimaced.

When I got involved with Soviet Jewry, our relationship improved noticeably. On the occasion when I refused to go to Moscow because the atmosphere was so negative, he sent a message of approval. As I've noted, Israel, and certainly the Begin government, took the position that all Soviet Jews traveling on Israeli visas when they exited the Soviet Union should go to Israel, instead of anywhere else, but we never let that stand between us. Until his death, I always spoke, however briefly, with Prime Minister Begin. Every time I was in Israel, I called Yehiel Kaddishai, his faithful number two, and I would have a few words. There is no question that the death of his wife saddened him deeply, and there's also no question in my mind that the actions of Arik Sharon and the massacres of Palestinians at Sabra and Shatilla caused him unbelievable heartache. Those events also caused him to resign, and new elections were called in the fall of 1982.

In that election, which pitted Yitzhak Shamir against Shimon Peres, the result was a tie. They made their own *cohabitation* and decided to split the four-year term into two—and Shimon Peres went first. He ran a supershow, pulled out of and ended the war in Lebanon, and as a result was able to cut inflation enormously, and the economy grew. But after his two years were done, he lived up to his word, and Shamir took over. I had a good relationship with Shamir and many chances to test his mettle—and I never found him wanting. For instance, the Greek Jewish community had proposed that I should visit the Greek Prime Minister and try to achieve full diplomatic relations between Greece and Israel. My team was urging me to go—after all, that's the stuff of news headlines and fund-raising. However, the Israeli Foreign Office wasn't so keen—they felt full relations would eventually happen; it wasn't at all crucial anyway, and why should they let me make them look bad? So I went to Mr. Shamir's office to discuss it. I could see that he really didn't want me to go, but he also didn't want to tell me *not* to go. I made it easy for him by telling him that if our places were reversed, *I* would tell me not to go—since his Foreign Ministry was against it. It was this same Shamir who kept confidential the news I gave him about Shevardnadze's pending CSCE proposals, and who supported me in the meetings and speeches in Berlin on the occasion of German reunification, despite criticism.

Of course, Shamir also did some things with which I strongly disagreed, chief of which was his continued insistence on settlement building in the occupied territories.

Indeed, the pace of such activity increased to an almost hysterical level in 1990 and 1991, just when they should not have. And in a paradoxical way, some of the responsibility for that can be laid at the feet of Shimon Peres.

Sometimes Shimon Peres reminds me of Nahum Goldmann. He is passionately devoted to peace, and has said on so many occasions that the Israeli soul cannot survive if Israelis are to be occupiers. At the first Plenum of my presidency of the WJC, he pointed out that it was the Diaspora's fault that Israel would have to give up most of the conquered territory, because we had stayed away in such droves, and that inclusion of the West Bank would make Israel a bi-national state and so lose its Jewish character. But he made one very serious tactical error in 1990. I was in his home in Tel Aviv one Friday night, and he and his close allies drew a picture of how they could pull down the National Unity government led by Shamir, with Rabin as Minister of Defense, and get some seventy-two seats for a Peres-led Labor Party government. I asked if they had discussed this with Rabin. They said no, seemingly puzzled, as if they thought he would have to go along. I replied that I was having dinner with the Defense Minister the following evening, and should they like, I would ask him. "Please do!" was the enthusiastic answer. I did, and Rabin's answer was no. He was getting along with Shamir, and the peace process was going along quite well, with Mubarak's help. I told the Peres people that they might dream of having seventy-two seats, but they didn't have a majority if they didn't have Rabin. Nevertheless, Shimon brought down the government with a vote of no confidence—and then found he couldn't form one of his own. He thought he could get most of the religious parties to come with him, but that turned out not to be the case. Those parties joined a new Shamir government, which became the most right-wing government in Israel's history. Shamir proceeded to build settlements like there was no tomorrow, really pissed off President George Bush, who was riding high after the Gulf War, and created new tensions in the territories.

———

The years 1990 and 1991 were, of course, the years of Desert Shield and Desert Storm, and the entire history of the Middle East changed within a very short time because of the presence of the United States forces, the demise of the Soviet Union, and the realignments within the Middle East itself.

Secretary of State James Baker's great success in putting together the coalition against Saddam Hussein's invasion of Kuwait was the high point of his career and the highwater mark for the United Nations. I think it is perfectly clear that if Iraq had been successful in annexing Kuwait, it would have been only a matter of months before Saudi Arabia was next. The world would have faced a nasty, arrogant dictator with a huge reserve of oil, who could easily have caused a crisis similar to the oil crisis of the Carter years.

A couple of things intrigue me about the Gulf War. For the first time since Israel's establishment, Arab fought Arab. In addition, America was desperately anxious to keep Israel out of it—this was also the first time that Israel was attacked and didn't retaliate. Assistant Secretary of State Lawrence Eagleburger was sent to Jerusalem to make sure that tough little Yitzhak Shamir didn't give in to his own instincts and retaliate as the Scuds were falling on Tel Aviv, but the truth of the matter was that the PM had a poll in his pocket that reported that a great percentage of the Israeli populace agreed that they should stay out. To placate the Israelis, the Bush administration sent the Patriot missiles to Israel, with technicians to operate them against the Scuds, another first. No American troops had ever fought side by side with Israelis before.

Our own personal contribution was that we held a meeting of the WJC Executive in Jerusalem in the middle of the struggle. We felt it necessary for world Jewry not only to show solidarity with Israel, but to do so physically. I remember the gas masks and the special room all ready in case of an attack, but I reasoned that the Iraqis would not be so stupid as to send their missiles anywhere near an Arab population—and Jerusalem has many Arab citizens—or near sacred sites, such as the Dome of the Rock. So I simply went to bed normally and ignored the Scuds. Others were not so lucky, though. The home near Tel Aviv of one of our executive members, Marcos Katz of Mexico City, was destroyed by a Scud.

I've said that George Bush, without necessarily meaning to be, was the best foreign friend Israel ever had—the only possible exception being Harry Truman, who recognized the state and made it legitimate. I get a lot of raised eyebrows with that. But let's examine the facts. With a telephone call, President Bush enabled all the Ethiopian Jews to be transported to Israel. Hundreds of millions of dollars were sent to Israel in compensation for damage done by Scuds (and as thanks for staying out of the war, and thus helping to keep the coalition together—the Syrians, certainly, and the Egyptians, probably, would have bolted had Israel joined in). The Gulf War incapacitated Israel's most implacable enemy. Iran is perhaps equally as hostile, but it is much farther away. The Bush administration got Arabs and Jews to sit down together for the first time since 1948 at the Madrid Conference, and I am proud that President Clinton acknowledged that fact at the historic White House signing of September 13, 1993. And while there was a deep malaise between President Bush and Prime Minister Shamir, the only actual evidence of that was Bush's refusal to guarantee billions of dollars of Israeli loans. (In 1992, after his election, Prime Minister Rabin invited Singer and me to a private luncheon at his suite in the Plaza Hotel prior to his going to Kennebunkport, Maine, for his first meeting with President Bush. I advised him that he would have no trouble with the loan guarantees now, as at that point in time, George Bush, who really liked and admired Rabin, needed the Israelis much more than the Israelis needed the American.)

One other important act committed by President Bush for Israel was the reversal of Resolution 3379 in the United Nations, which had equated Zionism with racism. I know a bit about how that happened, and I'd like to tell the story. It just might indicate how Hashem works his wonders, if you care to believe in the possibility of that sort of thing. Let me start at the beginning.

The Chairman of the United Nations Security Council during the month of December 1991 was the Ambassador of Romania. One day he called and said it was urgent that he see me. I called Israel Singer and asked him to be there at the meeting, and from him I learned that the Romanian Ambassador was a Jew. At the meeting, the Ambassador indicated that Boutros Boutros-Ghali was certain to be chosen as the new Secretary General, and that if we didn't act quickly, we might lose any chance of having "Zionism = Racism" canceled. He was convinced that, with an Egyptian as Secretary General, any attempt to undo Resolution 3379 was bound to be blocked. Just a few months before, in September, the President himself had addressed the United Nations and called for the rescinding of that resolution, so we knew he was on our side. But there was a Haman in the administration by the name of John Sununu, and he just happened to be the Chief of Staff. How to get the President?

A number of coincidences had to work to make the story happen. In the first place, the management at Tropicana, now owned by Seagram, happened to have a close relationship with the former Governor of Florida, who was now Bush's drug czar. Secondly, Bush was planning to make a trip to an industrial plant, and wanted to choose a drug-free environment, which Tropicana was, thanks to that former manager. Thirdly, Sununu happened to have been fired that very morning, or he would never have let me near enough to Mr. Bush to make my pitch. In fact, the former

New Hampshire Governor was fired on Air Force One on the way to Bradenton! When the President arrived at the Tropicana facility, not only was I there to greet him, but Sununu was shown to a private office, where he cooled his heels.

The President greeted me warmly, and I had to find the right time to make my pitch. That came on a "walk through the warehouse." The local manager was with us, and as he was about to say something, I nudged him and asked the President if I could discuss something that had nothing to do with his trip. He answered in the affirmative. I proceeded:

"Mr. President, this might be a perfect time to iterate your stand on the rescinding of Zionism equals racism in the United Nations. It might help get Prime Minister Shamir out of the tree he's in. We have counted the votes, and we are sure we shall win. The worst-case scenario is a twenty-vote margin, and the best some fifty." (Actually, we did much better than that.)

"But, Edgar, I thought that was all taken care of."

"Mr. President, as of this morning, Ambassador Pickering told the World Jewish Congress that he is uninstructed on this matter."

The President stopped in his tracks. "Edgar, would you

please repeat that!" It sounded more like a command than a request.

"Yes, sir. As of this morning, Ambassador to the United Nations Thomas Pickering allowed as to the fact that he had no instructions on the matter of Resolution 3379."

"Thank you, Edgar." And I knew we had won. After the ceremonies, a plaque for being a drug-free plant, and the necessary speeches, the President retired to an office we had made available, as per a White House request. I went to another office, where Tropicana executives were hanging out. In about twenty minutes, it was Israel Singer on the telephone.

"Edgar, what's going on down there?"

"Why, Israel?"

"Why, because Margaret Tutwiler has just appeared on the steps of the State Department and said that Pickering has been instructed to put a full-court press on reversing the Zionism-equals-racism resolution."

———

The election of 1992 was, of course, won by Rabin. On a Saturday that spring, before the election, Steve Herbits, Executive Vice President of Seagram in Charge of Public Affairs, and I went to pay a call on Yitzhak Rabin in his Tel Aviv apartment. My first impressions of Mr. Rabin had totally changed. We sat in his library, and I was very impressed with his plans. Although for political purposes he couldn't discuss privatization—Histadrut, the huge labor union, was too important a voting block to antagonize—his understanding of economics was impressive and his plans for peace were strategically perfect, as were all his strategies. Right there and then, I decided to back him. When it was quite clear that he had won, Uri Savir, then Consul General in New York and soon to be the Director General of the Foreign Office, called me and said that with the exception of his own wife, I was the first person he had called to announce the news, as I was the first person that he had known to come out solidly for Yitzhak Rabin. I had not only supplied funds myself, but I had held a dinner for him in New York—he had spoken very effectively and said very kind things about me—which had been quite successful in raising funds. I don't like to give money to Israeli political parties, but I felt that in this case we had a real chance for peace should Rabin win, and not Likud.

My brother and I and our wives were at the White House ceremony on September 13, 1993, to watch the handshake that changed the Middle East forever. I heard Yitzhak Rabin

deliver the speech of his life. And I was there at his funeral.

On the morning of the signing, we all got up very early,
and were in place on the White House lawn between eight-
thirty and eight forty-five. The ceremony itself was scheduled
to begin at eleven o'clock, and was about ten minutes late.
No matter. We watched history being made, and throughout
the entire ceremony we were all in a state of euphoria—the
dream of peace in the Middle East seemed to be coming true.

The official program contained the following words on
the facing page: ". . . it is time to put an end to decades of
confrontation and conflict, recognize their mutual legitimate
and political rights, and strive to live in peaceful coexistence
and mutual dignity and security, and achieve a just, lasting, and comprehensive peace settlement and historic reconciliation through the agreed political process," and was identi-
fied as "Excerpts from the Declaration of Principles on
Interim Self-Government Arrangements."

President Clinton spoke first. He mentioned the Camp
David accords, and paid tribute to Jimmy Carter, who was
there in the first row. He then went on to the Madrid
meeting, the first time Israelis and Arabs other than Egyptians had ever talked to each other since Camp David, and
paid tribute to George Bush, also there in the first row. He

proceeded to pledge the cooperation of the United States in the negotiations to come.

Next came Shimon Peres. We all expected him to give the speech of his life, but he was barely adequate. What a pity, since he, more than anyone, had navigated the shoals to bring that ship into harbor. He was followed by Mahmoud Abbas, a member of the executive committee of the PLO, who spoke in Arabic (which was translated) and didn't say much, but at considerable length. Then came the actual signing. First Peres, then Abbas, then Kozyrev, Minister of Foreign Affairs of the Russian Federation, and Warren Christopher, both as witnesses and co-sponsors of the peace process.

Then there were more speeches. Warren Christopher was short and correct and said the right things, which everyone expected him to do. Then came Andrei Kozyrev, who spoke off the cuff, and more or less said that he was glad that the Israelis were talking to the secularist PLO because the fundamentalists, both religious and political, were a bunch of bastards, and were making his life miserable. He wanted peace not just in the Middle East, but in the entire region, meaning Afghanistan, Iran, etc.

Then came Yitzhak Rabin. He stole the show! He was magnificent! He spoke from the heart, and he was moved, and so very moving. He started out by saying how difficult this was. He talked of the pain, of the mothers grieving for their sons and daughters, of war and the bloodshed he knew as an old soldier; he talked about terrorism and murder, and then he talked about peace. "Enough" became his thrust. "Enough" of pain and suffering, enough of war and bloodshed, *enough*. He built the emotion of the moment and explained why he was daring to make peace with the PLO. Because there had to be an end to killing, to war. Our children and their children had to have a chance to lead a normal life. He ended with a prayer and asked the audience to join him: ". . . let Him make peace, for us and for all Israel, and let us say, Amen." He got some ovation!

Then came the man with the *shmate* on his head, but no gun on his hip. Yasir Arafat was good enough, and we must remember that he was talking to his constituency as much as to the audience. When he finished, there was a round of handshaking, and everyone watched to see whether or not Rabin would shake Arafat's hand. He did, but with obvious physical reluctance—his body involuntarily recoiled as his hand went forward. One could see him making up his mind. It took President Clinton's physical urging to make that hand reach Arafat's. The entire 3,000 people rose as one and cheered!

President Clinton's conclusion was moving. He spoke of the trumpets that had once brought down the walls of Jericho. Now they were breaking down the walls of hatred and enmity, and Jericho would once more flourish. Good symbolism. According to the agreement, Jericho would be returned to Palestinian rule. The White House had cleverly brought a group of Palestinian children and a group of Israeli children to sit together in the front rows. It was absolutely fantastic to be there at an event that would change the history of the Middle East forever.

Not everybody was pleased, of course. Benjamin "Bibi" Netanyahu of Likud saw fit to write an article for the op-ed page of the *New York Times*, criticizing the Oslo accord and likening it to Chamberlain's Munich Pact in 1938. The headline was "Peace in Our Time?" I thought that someone ought to make a reply, and then I decided that someone should be me, so I wrote:

To the Editor:

I am disappointed by "Peace in Our Time?" Benjamin Netanyahu's criticism of the Israel–Palestine Liberation Organization peace plan as comparable to Neville Chamberlain's appeasement of Hitler over Czechoslovakia.

During the Menachem Begin–Yitzhak Shamir years,

Mr. Netanyahu's Likud Party was the most ardent pro-moter of the unwritten rule that American Jews who dis-agreed with Israeli government policy should voice their disagreement in Israel, not in United States forums. Now Mr. Netanyahu seeks to make an end run on the Labor Party by contravening the spirit of that rule.

He ignores the many instances when American Jews were lectured to, pilloried, or given the cold shoulder by Likud for voicing criticism of plans to annex the West Bank and efforts to expand Israeli settlements in occupied territories. Now that Mr. Netanyahu is out of power, he seems not to mind the double standard.

The substance of Mr. Netanyahu's article also irks me. Yitzhak Rabin's Labor Party was elected on the promise of bringing peace to Israel. It is on the verge of doing that, and the plan it offers is as prudent as it is bold. There are nu-merous safeguards against terrorist recidivism, should the PLO be unable to govern. To compare it to the appeasement of Hitler is beyond hyperbole—it is hysteria. One almost has the impression that Mr. Netanyahu is more concerned that the peace will succeed than fail, thereby strengthening the Labor Party's hold on the government and keeping Mr. Netanyahu from becoming prime minister. One wonders if the timing and style of Mr. Netanyahu's argument isn't

motivated by self-interest at odds with the national interest
of the Israeli people.

Edgar M. Bronfman

In June of 1995, I was once again in Jerusalem. I had traveled from New York to Jerusalem via Taiwan, China, and India, and the Rabins had a dinner in honor of my birthday on the roof of their Tel Aviv apartment. His toast was so warm, and to make sure I understood that this was personal, only members of his family were at our table. I spoke with him that evening about the naysayers in America who seemed to be trying to kill the peace process based on a false sense that there was a lack of security. I insisted on the need to have competent army officers ready to refute those stupid arguments. When it comes to security, I said, the American Jewish community must be told by those with the proper credentials, "Trust Yitzhak Rabin. I do."

Five months later, I was at his funeral.

On the afternoon of November 4, 1995, I was sitting at my desk in Charlottesville, Virginia, studying I Kings, when the telephone rang and my son, Matthew, who was in Jerusalem, told me that Yitzhak Rabin had been shot. I was shocked, and then furious, and then so terribly sad. When I found out about a half hour later that the killer was a Jew, my disgust was overwhelming. I had to scream out my anger at a Jew who could so pervert our glorious religion as to boast that God had told him to kill Mr. Rabin because he was about to give Israel over to the Arabs. I called him a loathsome, arrogant cockroach. He demeaned every Jew in the world with his murderous act.

I equally condemn those now who called for the slaying of Yitzhak Rabin, those hysterical ideologues who pervert Judaism with their total disregard for life, as they scream for the death of those who seek peace. It's hard to understand the total amorality of those messianists who think that they are in tune with the messianic clock, that they know that the arrival of the Messiah is imminent, and that Israel and the Jewish people must own all of *eretz Yisrael* or the Messiah will refuse to appear. Even Joshua got sick of killing and failed to conquer all the land, and it is clear that, while the land of Israel is holy, life is that much more holy. When I think of rabbis who also call for the death of the "traitors" who would lead the sons of Israel down the beautiful road to peace, I get sick to my stomach. A rabbi who would advocate that a man be put to death should be instantly excommunicated, at the very least. I loathe and despise those Israelis who would dare to call Rabin a traitor, and I abhor those who depicted him

in the uniform of a Waffen SS officer. These "characteriza-
tions" were exhibited at Likud rallies, and just as at Sabra and
Shatilla, where the court ruled that Israeli eyes saw, they could
have prevented the massacre and did not—which made them
equally guilty—so I must characterize the Likud leadership,
who witnessed this disgusting travesty, whose eyes saw and
who did nothing to prevent it, and who have their share of
responsibility and guilt.

My wife, Jan, and I flew that afternoon to Westchester
County Airport, just outside of New York City, where we
picked up Evelyne and Israel Singer, Elan Steinberg, and Ron
Lauder, and flew overnight to Jerusalem.

As you can imagine, security was tight in Jerusalem the
morning we landed. Thanks to some great organization on
the ground by Dr. Avi Beker, the Executive Director of the
Israel branch of the WJC, and his team, we had an army es-
cort to the hotel. After a wash following an all-night flight,
we set out for the cemetery and the ceremony.

Mount Herzl, dominated by Herzl's grave in black stone,
is the site of the graves of all the prime ministers and great
Zionist leaders, including my beloved predecessor, Nahum
Goldmann, and there the authorities had erected a large out-
door amphitheater. My card had a circle on it, which meant
special seating, as did Israel Singer's, and so we were able to

watch as the heads of state and government filed in to pay homage to the memory of Yitzhak Rabin. They were all there: from North America, Prime Minister Chrétien of Canada and President Clinton. From Europe, Jacques Chirac, President of France; Felipe Gonzales, Prime Minister of Spain; Chancellor Kohl of Germany; Prince Charles of the United Kingdom, as well as Prime Minister Major; the Prime Minister of the Russian Federation; Prime Minister Gyula Horn of Hungary; Chancellor Franz Vranitzky of Austria, and on and on. Some eighty-five countries were represented in all, including many from Africa and Asia.

What a tribute, I thought to myself: what a tribute to a great man, to Israel and to the Jewish people. Because, I reflected, Israel is on the way to peace and prosperity for the entire region, winning respect and support in so doing. Five thousand people were there, but what transcended the size of that audience was the size of the crowd that came to Jerusalem Saturday night—a million and a half souls, 25 percent of the Jewish population of Israel. What galvanized the people to express their love to Yitzhak Rabin, their scorn of the right-wing-dog killer mechanism? Perhaps it was their longing for peace and their trust in a great soldier, a great statesman, and a great leader. As I was told later, they felt they had lost a father, and the whole country grieved as it never had before.

The ceremony began with the wail of a loud, mournful siren. For two minutes, it wailed, and it set the mood for the afternoon. Then there was an honor guard befitting a great soldier, and the speeches began. President Ezer Weizman began, and unfortunately, winged it and was less than presidential. King Hussein of Jordan made a regal and most important speech. He referred to Leah Rabin as his sister—most important in the Arab world—and to Yitzhak as his brother. He was followed by Shimon Peres, who was very good, especially when one considers that not so long ago he and Rabin had been enemies, until they both decided they needed each other to make their dreams of peace a reality. He was followed by President Clinton. I almost burst with pride in my President. He spoke with feeling, sensitivity, and humility, the best speech I've ever heard him give. He ended with "*Shalom, chaver*," as he had in his speech in the Rose Garden when he'd heard the awful news. There were already bumper stickers throughout Israel with that slogan.

Felipe Gonzales, Prime Minister of Spain, spoke for the European Community, and was followed by Boutros Boutros-Ghali, Secretary General of the United Nations. He was followed by the Prime Minister of the Russian Federation, and then it got more personal. Shimon Sheves, Yitzhak Rabin's right-hand man and lately in charge of the political campaign to come, spoke with a depth of feeling that was out-done only by Yitzhak's granddaughter, Noa Ben-Artzi Filosof, who said that she wasn't there to talk about peace, but about her grandfather, whom she obviously loved very deeply. For-tunately, my friend Liliane Shalom, who was a part of the Mo-roccan delegation, was sitting near me and had a big supply of Kleenex. I needed some, as my tears flowed. Noa's speech was reprinted in the *Jerusalem Post* the next morning. I read it and cried once more.

She was followed by the Director General of the Prime Minister's office, Etan Haber, who had with him the square of paper that Rabin had tucked into his shirt pocket, containing the words of the song to peace he had been trying to sing—Haber said that while his Prime Minister did so many things so well, singing was not one of them—the words blurred by Yitzhak's blood. Perhaps a bit melodramatic, but I did understand his passion.

From the amphitheater, the heads of state and VIPs went to the gravesite. There we had a chance to shake hands with the members of the American delegation that President Clin-ton had brought with him, the leadership of Congress, ex-Presidents Carter and Bush, and leaders of American Jewish organizations. Everybody was there saying good-bye.

All Monday night long, people came to the gravesite, a

cross section of the populace, to pay respects because they felt they had to. The vigil continued throughout Tuesday and Tuesday night, people lying down around the grave, no one saying anything but prayers, others leaving written messages in nearby cracks in the wall, as people do at the Wall of the Temple.

Tuesday, I met with Shimon Peres, and we discussed his determination to carry on, to finish the job he and Yitzhak Rabin had set out to do. I wished him well and prayed for his success. Perhaps, we agreed, the country will have learned a lesson. Perhaps they will understand that peace is the only answer.

Tuesday afternoon we called on Leah Rabin. It was very difficult getting to her apartment building. Thousands of people were in the streets, standing a solemn watch, and thousands of candles were winking in the dusk of a winter afternoon. Traffic was at a standstill, but we were able to approach on foot through side streets, and we were taken up on the very inadequate elevator to the penthouse apartment, where hundreds of people stood in the halls, dining and living rooms, all anxious to express their sympathy. As we were ushered into the library where I had sat so often with Yitzhak, Crown Prince Hassan was on her right, and I was seated on her left. It seemed normal that His Royal Highness would be there offering comfort to the grieving widow. How that part of the world has changed. Oh, that something good like peace and prosperity will come out of that dastardly murder!

When I took my leave, I hugged Leah and told her that I loved her and had really loved her husband. She replied, "He loved you too, and he respected you." That almost made me cry again. She is brave and strong, but, oh, when shivah was over, I knew she'd be lonely. I wonder if murderers ever think of the families of their victims.

I really loved Yitzhak Rabin. I miss him personally, and will miss him as a leader. He was infinitely brave, infinitely strong, and infinitely wise in his decision to try to end the bloodshed of half a century and fight for peace. We can't let that battle die with him. Blessed be the peacemakers!

And so I said farewell to a great statesman, a great soldier, with the words of President Clinton: "*Shalom, chaver.*"

On my way home, the idea came to me for the rally in Madison Square Garden to galvanize the American Jewish community. A few short weeks later, it was a reality.

Let me explain just how I feel about the peace process that seems to be so divisive, both in Israel and here in the United States. It is being castigated by the right-wingers and their allies as too risky, that Israel's security cannot stand a Palestinian state on its border—it would be like a dagger pointed straight at the country's heart. Yes, the Hamas bombings in Tel Aviv and Jerusalem have been horrible, revolting, almost unimaginable. But I still believe that one of the best things that could happen to Israel is to have a democratic Palestinian state on its border. That democracy will spread to Jordan, in time to Iraq, and to the Arabian peninsula. To those who say that the words *Arab* and *democracy* are mutually exclusive, I say nonsense. There are elections in the West Bank, despite the opposition of Hamas. Their democracy may soon be real.

There are no other choices that make sense. Should Israel annex the West Bank to be part of a bi-national state? Or should Israel annex the West Bank but practice apartheid by withholding political participation from the Palestinians? Unthinkable. Should it insist on the status quo and return to the *intifada* and the filthy work of occupation, of breaking bones and beating up kids? I was asked to discuss the assassination of Yitzhak Rabin with a bunch of eight-year-old girls at my granddaughter's school. I explained that it was as if the two of them had been fighting for years and years over the same piece of carpet. They had kicked and punched each other, pulled each other's hair, and finally they had gotten sick of fighting and decided to see if there was a way to share the carpet. As their discussions began, a friend of one, who thought that God rested upon the whole carpet, decided her friend could not give any of it away, and killed her. Surely working for peace is God's work. And let us not forget that the IDF is the most powerful fighting force in the region, and isn't going to disappear.

Another important point is that maintenance of the integrity of the Golan Heights is absolutely essential for Israel's security. That strategic territory cannot be abandoned without enormous assurances that any movement by Syrian troops will be known through sophisticated monitoring equipment. I believe that the United States should have technicians on the Golan Heights to operate that equipment, and to reassure the Israeli populace that there is no danger from any sneak Syrian attack, or from shellings, as there were before 1967.

But there are those fanatics who believe that they are in touch with the messianic time schedule, and they are convinced that he is due momentarily. But, they scream in their zealotry, he will not come if Jews are not in control of the entire biblical *eretz Yisrael*. I don't know how to deal with zealots, with totally unreasoning people—of the stripe that assassinated Yitzhak Rabin. Surely the rhetoric will die down. Surely the Netanyahus, the Benny Begins, and Meridors, sane oppositionists, will no longer sit quietly by while the crazy zealots harangue Likud rallies and cast heroes as Nazis, screaming that they should be killed.

And surely peace will come. If it gives the indigenous peoples of the region a better standard of life, if the light at the end of the tunnel brings a measure of prosperity, and is not a train coming at them, then peace has a very good chance of lasting. Amen.

CHAPTER 10

NEW DIRECTIONS

In the early 1960s, my father said that if I thought that anti-Semitism was dead, I was fooling myself.

At that time, I really believed it was all but dead, that in the aftermath of the Holocaust, being anti-Semitic would be out of fashion forever. And so it is in many parts of the United States and Canada. There are pockets of hate throughout the world, and unfortunately we live in a racist society, and that will take many millennia to change.

In too many parts of the world, however, this nastiness has been cropping up and getting worse. Even in places where there are few Jews, there can be virulent anti-Semitism.

One has but to think of the last election in Poland, where distinctions were made between "real Poles" and "others."

At the Plenary Assembly of the WJC in Jerusalem in January 1991, we reached a decision to create a commission on anti-Semitism, and that group decided to hold a meeting in July 1992 in Brussels to examine anti-Semitism, racism, and xenophobia.

This international conference was called "My Brother's Keeper." The questions before us were how to promote the positive aspects of three forces—nationalism, ethnicity, and religion—and how to prevent them from becoming destructive.

There are two rather droll stories I should like to relate about the conference. The first concerns President Mitterrand of France. We picked an unfortunate day to visit with him, two days after the electorate had handed his party its head. We were discussing the Middle East and the Arab boycott of Israeli and Jewish goods, and to try to lighten up the atmosphere, I started to tell him an amusing story concerning Seagram. It had to do with Mumm Champagne, and so I started with, "You understand, Mr. President, that Seagram owns Mumm Champagne." Before I could go any further, he interrupted, saying in a gruff voice, "And Martell, too."

I went on with the story anyway.

"Some years ago, when we owned only twenty-five percent of Mumm, the company received an order from Egypt for one thousand cases. With the order came a questionnaire, obviously meant to ascertain Jewish ownership, which asked: just how much of Seagram did Mumm own? It was, of course, badly phrased, but dutifully the answer was delivered: 'None.'

"Then the people in the bottling department evidently didn't know the difference between Arabic script and Hebrew, and instead of the mandatory Arabic back label, they adhered Hebrew ones. That could have been a grave error—but not one bottle was returned. So much for anti-Jewish diligence!"

Even the dour Mitterrand had to smile.

The other story concerned George Bush. In late April of 1992, Steve Herbits and I were at the White House for what we thought would be a major policy address by Lamar Alexander, the Secretary of Education, on innovative ways of teaching in elementary and high schools. It wasn't quite up to its billing, but after Alexander's presentation, the President took the podium and then received the audience halfway between the East Room and the West Room, where cocktails were to be served. As Steve and I passed through the line, Mr. Bush said "Gee, Edgar, it's good to see you," with a big smile.

He then turned to Mrs. Bush and said, "You remember Edgar," and Barbara said, "Of course I know Edgar." His tone made me think that he probably didn't know many people there, and so I decided to take advantage of his gracious welcome. I positioned myself in the West Room, so that when he entered he would see me first. I was lucky and he made a beeline for me. I asked permission to discuss what I thought was a good election opportunity, and he nodded, so I proceeded.

I remarked that the situation between Israel and the United States wasn't at all good. I said that in the past, previous presidents who had had a problem with the Israeli government used to make speeches about Soviet Jewry, and American Jews would then understand that the problem was about a particular act by the Israeli government, but that the administration was still to be trusted as not being anti-Semitic or anti-Israel. No such speech was possible now, but one thing Jews always responded to was anti-Semitism. He encouraged me to continue, and so I mentioned the upcoming Brussels meeting on anti-Semitism, racism, and xenophobia in July. I went on to say that I knew he couldn't be there, as he would be totally occupied with the meeting of the G-7 in Munich. But, said I, if the First Lady could make a speech representing the President, and deploring all sorts of racism and bias, then it could have a good effect, and because of the time change, it would play on the evening news on American television that same day. The fact that the appearance was in Europe would also make it non-pandering.

He seemed enthusiastic, and called to Mrs. Bush, "Hey, Bar, come over here" (after all, he was the President, and she had served broccoli, which she must have known he hated), and asked me to repeat what I had just said. I thought he'd move away while I talked, but no, he stayed right where he was. I repeated what I had just said to him, with a little more detail, and when I was through, the President turned to the First Lady and said, "That sounds good for us." Mrs. Bush summoned her executive secretary, and it seemed all buttoned up when she said, "All right, write me a good speech and make sure there's a joke in it."

Herbits and I, accompanied by her executive secretary, went to our car, we exchanged dates and cards, and then we proceeded to write the speech. And that's the last I heard of it. Months later, I was having a drink with Secretary of State Lawrence Eagleburger, a friend and neighbor in Charlottesville, Virginia. He asked if I were interested in knowing why Mrs. Bush hadn't come to Brussels. He proceeded to tell me that he had liked the idea, Scowcroft had liked the idea, but when Barbara had gotten with her claque, *they* had decided that it was too much trouble, too far away (less than an hour by air from Munich!), and, anyway, it wasn't in the United States.

Before the conference, I had gone out on a limb by asking the Reverend Jesse Jackson, one of America's outstanding African-Americans, to participate. I believed then, as I believe now, that Jesse Jackson is a moderate. Jesse preaches learning, education, self-improvement, hard work, and pride to black America, and works like a tiger for those goals. He even travels from school to school trying to get kids to give up on guns and drugs, and to snitch on those who use either.

I invited the Reverend Mr. Jackson for three reasons. First, I had read an op-ed piece in the *New York Times* by A. M. Rosenthal on a speech Jesse had given in California, in which he had reached out to the Jews (Rosenthal's column had been somewhat critical, but basically positive). Second, I thought a conference with the word *racism* in its title could not afford to omit racism in America, and I couldn't think of anyone who could address that problem so well. Third, I had met Jesse on many occasions, and I had learned to trust his integrity and his real feelings toward the Jewish people.

Some years ago, months after the "Hymie" incident, when Jesse had been heard to refer to New York City as "Hymie-town," he and his son Jesse, Jr., now a member of the House of Representatives, and an aide had come to lunch at the Seagram offices. Israel Singer, Steve Herbits, and Elan Steinberg also had been present. As we sat down at the table, I turned to Jesse and said, "You may not want to discuss this, but I'd like to bring up the 'Hymie' incident."

Jesse groaned. "Must you?"

I said, "Jesse, wait until I'm through, and then tell me whether or not it was worthwhile."

"OK, go ahead," said Jesse.

"We all know that you were a couple of weeks too late when you made your apology. Forget that. I just want to suggest what you might have said at the beginning of your remarks. You might have said, 'Before I apologize, and I will, I would like everyone in this synagogue who has never called a member of my race a *shvartser* to stand up.' That would have put your use of the word 'Hymie' in the proper context."

Jesse looked a bit shocked, then smiled and said, "Why didn't I think of that?"

"Because you're a *shvartser*," came my instant response. He roared with laughter.

I expected a lot of criticism, and I got it. Simcha Dinitz,

then Chairman of the Executive of the World Zionist Organization and of the Jewish Agency, was very indignant, and refused to attend the conference, until I told him that I was taking his attitude personally, and would not accept his position. He came, if only for a short time. Abe Foxman, National Director of the Anti-Defamation League of B'nai B'rith, also gave us a hard time, but he relented and was a strong contributor to the conference.

Jesse Jackson took his assignment seriously. He consulted with Rabbi Alexander Schindler, head of the Reform movement in America; with Elie Wiesel, the Nobel laureate who also made a great contribution to the conference; with Israel Singer and Elan Steinberg; and when he made his speech, he was very good. He strongly advocated renunciation of all forms of racism, including the anti-Semitism of black America. His presence and his speech sparked the possibility that the trend of bad relations between the Jewish and African-American communities might be reversed, that once again we could form an alliance for the betterment of both groups.

I heard from Reverend Jackson after the conference, and we agreed to plan a series of meetings throughout the country, where we and others would engage in dialogue and help launch the new relationship. Unfortunately, Jesse's schedule is somewhat unstructured. He moves from crisis to crisis, doing good, but I cannot work on such an ad hoc basis, and we have yet to put our plan into action. My staff has tried to work through this, and while the spirit has been willing, the right format eludes us.

Press coverage for the conference was excellent. The *New York Times* carried the Jesse Jackson story on the front page, and the Monday after we returned from the conference, it devoted the entire op-ed page to an article written by Harvard professor Henry Louis Gates, Jr., on the subject of black/Jewish relations, based on Jesse Jackson's appearance in Brussels.

My hope, which I often expressed during the conference, is that nations worldwide, faced with outbreaks of nationalist, religious, and ethnic wars, in what was the Soviet Union, in Yugoslavia, in Africa, the Far East, and Lebanon, will call for an international conference, such as the one held on the environment in 1992 in Rio de Janeiro, to devise strategies for preventing the slaughters that result from these chauvinistic struggles. Our conference might be the precursor. Unfortunately, this has not yet happened.

But I must confess that my attention has been diverted. I don't really believe that overt anti-Semitism is the biggest threat facing the Jewish world, not by a long shot. The fact of the matter is that the world is a better place for Jews than it has ever been, so good that we are being accepted into the general society at an alarming rate. Our more recent history is not as it was in the past: we have not just left the misery of the Pale of Settlement to come to America (or elsewhere) to be better Jews but, in effect, to escape our Judaism. That's the real threat: a history that teaches us that, by and large, from a physical standpoint, it wasn't so great to be Jewish; an open society that greets us mostly with a welcome smile; and at least two generations of Jews who knew nothing of their religion. For too many years, we have expressed ourselves, not by learning Judaism and the pride that comes from that, but by writing checks for Israel and feeling pride in that country and its mighty army. We face extinction in the Diaspora, that's the real threat.

In the Diaspora, I see a slight reversal in the trend to assimilation. There was a time when Jews tried hard not to be Jews, and hoped the world would accept them as such. There is a story about a man named Levy who applied to join a country club. As they refused his membership, it was carefully explained that they did not accept Jews. All right, he thought, I'll fix that. He changed his last name to Lloyd, joined an Anglican church, and began dressing like a proper WASP. Two years later, he reapplied for admission to the country club. Everything was going well until the chairman of the board of admissions asked him about his religion. "*Goy!*" he answered proudly.

Today, however, nationalism has come to be a force, and even more than that, increasing numbers of people have started learning about their roots and taking pride in them. Alex Haley's book, flawed though it may be, has been an example of that force.

I continue to insist that the fight against anti-Semitism must be fought on two levels. First, it must be exposed for the sick behavior that it is. Second, Jews must take pride in their Jewishness. But you can't be proud of a heritage of which you know nothing. This means, essentially, that Jews must have a better Jewish education.

Richard Joel, the head of International Hillel, an organization that serves Jewish youth on college campuses, has said that being "chosen" is no longer enough, Jews must now become "choosing." Our religion has a great philosophical grounding, marvelous traditions, and a great body of lore. But if Jewish continuity is to become a reality in the Diaspora, we must "choose" to learn to communicate it or, to put it in business terms, to "market" it effectively. This is one of the great tasks that lie ahead for all of us, and it is of particular concern to the Jewish federations throughout the United States and Canada. It is also of particular concern to me, not least because of my own personal failings in earlier years.

I am now sure that if I had had more conviction, Ann would have agreed to give the children as much Jewish education as I wanted them to have. But I was ambivalent. Part of my great eagerness to marry was to get out from under my father, and this certainly included my upbringing—my Jewishness.

I followed the path of least resistance. I made no effort to have our children learn anything about their traditions as Jews. I joined neither a synagogue nor a temple. My Jewishness all but lapsed. But never for a second did I forget that I was a Jew, and when I came to work for Seagram in New York City, it was natural for me to involve myself in corporate fund-raising for the Federation of Jewish Philanthropies and for the United Jewish Appeal.

The creation of the State of Israel affected me as it affected other Jews. I took pride in the accomplishment of David Ben-Gurion and his army of Jewish patriots, so undersupplied in wherewithal, but so blessedly oversupplied in bravery and determination. And when the Six-Day War came and went, there was, generally speaking, even more pride, and a kind of euphoria about being Jewish and supporting the Jewish State. That certainly included me.

My Jewish awareness grew during the fifties and sixties, and bubbled over after my father's death. I traveled once more to Israel, this time not as a hanger-on, but as a principal, as one of Father's heirs. And shortly thereafter, I began to get involved in the World Jewish Congress.

My religious awakenings developed much more slowly, and even today, no practicing Jew would pay much heed to the knowledge I've acquired. But still, the religion fascinates me, and I do study. That day with Israel Singer on the aircraft headed for Moscow was a seed that bore some fruit. I remember being amazed that thousands of Russian Jews would gather around Moscow's Choral Synagogue every Simchat Torah. How, I wondered, did they know the date? How could a religion survive three generations of proscription? So I started to read the Bible. My mentor, Singer, gave me the Stone edition of the Chamash, the Five Books of Moses, which has marvelous commentary. Every now and then, I send Israel e-mail messages asking for more explanation, or arguing with the interpretation. The more I learn, the prouder I become of my heritage. The Bible is our book, our story, and not only is it fascinating in and of itself, it also gives me an identity—that of a proud Jew!

I am grateful that Jan likes having Sabbath service at the table on Friday nights, even if it is *de minimis*. I truly enjoy the seder service at my table, where some of my children and grandchildren sit, and where I try to explain parts of the service that are the most meaningful to me. I always pause over the passage where it is written that the angels laughed as the Red Sea came back to drown the pursuing Egyptians, and the Lord was angry with them: "Do not laugh, for those, too, are my children." I point out that every Jew must learn tolerance from these lines. I also point out that it is written, "Love the stranger, for you were a stranger in the land of Egypt."

After my divorce from Ann, I was married for a while to an Englishwoman named Rita Webb, whom we called George. We had two children together: Sara, born on November 21, 1976, and Clare, born on April 8, 1979. I've not been very successful in teaching Sara and Clare about their background, but Clare, who now lives with me in Virginia, has decided that she's a Jew. She loves the Friday-night service as we do, and hopefully she'll become more involved as time passes.

Their mother converted just before Sara was born, and we were remarried in a synagogue, but after the divorce, George reverted to being a non-practicing member of the Church of England, and the girls spent their time in England's Suffolk County, far from any Jewish educational facility.

Shortly before her fourteenth birthday, Clare faced overt anti-Semitism for the first time. During a telephone call from

England, where she then lived, I asked if she was happy at school, and she said, "Well, sort of."

When I asked her to tell me about it, she said she was being kidded about being American, or half-American. I knew this couldn't be all that upsetting, so asked, "And about being Jewish, or half-Jewish?"

She then started to cry, and admitted this was so. It's always tough the first time it happens, and you never get used to it, but you have to learn to live with it. I did the best I could over the telephone, and then wrote her a letter to be delivered the next day, telling her that I was shocked at what had happened to her, but that I wasn't surprised. I described my first encounter with anti-Semitism for her, when I had worked as a caddy at the golf course in Ste. Marguerite in Canada.

I told her that this had happened during World War II, when millions of Jews were being systematically slaughtered by the Nazis, in what we now call the Holocaust, and when the good people of the world were fighting the Nazis, and all the democracies were embattled, trying to defeat Hitler and company. Even so, overt anti-Semitism was still there in Ste. Marguerite, and I had been told that I was not welcome to play at a club if I brought my relatives who looked too Jewish.

I had survived that episode, I told her, but it had left a scar, which turned into a determination to fight all kinds of prejudice wherever it existed. With a name like Bronfman, I said, she will always be considered a Jew, and she would have to get used to that. The worst thing she could do would be to deny her Jewish heritage, because it would eventually make her hate herself. The only way for a Jew to fight anti-Semitism is to recognize that to be a Jew is to have a great heritage, and to expose anti-Semites for what they are—evil, vicious, stupid, and insecure.

Clare got through this first experience because of the timely intervention of her headmaster, whom I called immediately, and who counseled her wisely (according to Clare, he also expelled the student who had taunted her and who had a history of persecuting classmates). Perhaps this incident made her decide to be Jewish. The more she learns about her Jewish heritage, the stronger she'll become. I really believe that.

Clare is the youngest of my seven children. The oldest is Sam, born October 23, 1953, who married Melanie Mann. She was absolutely devoted to her church, which was Episcopal, and Sam adopted her religion as his own. She died of breast cancer in December 1991, and made Sam promise to bring up their two children in that same religion. He will honor that vow. Nevertheless, he also plays a major role in Jewish charities in the San Francisco Jewish community.

Edgar, Jr., born May 16, 1955, knows full well that he is Jewish. His first wife, an African-American named Sherry Brewer, is a Buddhist, and he is now married to the former Clarissa Alcock, from Venezuela. Her family is Catholic, but they both insisted that a rabbi be present along with the priest at their Caracas wedding. His son from his previous marriage, Benjamin Zachary, was bar mitzvahed in December 1995 at the Park Avenue Synagogue, which is Conservative. He read his portion in Hebrew, and I followed it, and he made not one mistake. I was very proud of him. His mother also participated in the service, since she is totally supportive of Ben's decision to be Jewish.

Holly, born August 28, 1956, has a real need for spirituality, and she toyed with various gurus until she discovered that Judaism has all the spirituality she could hope to find. She is, for all intents and purposes, *shomer shabbat*, a keeper of the Sabbath, and is extremely well read in her religion. She is also very active in her temple in Charlottesville, and with the local Hillel at the University of Virginia.

Matthew, born July 16, 1959, first married Fiona Wood, also Catholic. They brought up their children—Jeremy, Eli, and Gabriela—as Jews. In fact, since Fiona's mother is very religious, and because Fiona didn't want to convert to Judaism, Matthew took the two boys to a shul in Stamford and did a ceremony with them in the mikvah so that, according to Israel Singer, their Judaism could never be questioned. He is now married to Lisa Belzberg, and they both are Orthodox.

Adam, born March 22, 1963, is married to Cindy Gage, and they have four children: Joshua, Zachary, Samantha, and Jacob. They belong to the Stephen Wise Synagogue in Los Angeles, and their children will be Jewish in the Reform tradition. Adam was the only son of mine to be bar mitzvahed, and I give credit to my then wife, George, for urging him to do that, while she was going through the process of converting to Judaism.

I have no idea what religion Sara will finally choose. She has gone through the normal phase of rebellion, especially from her mother, but she certainly knows that she is Jewish—as I said to Clare, with a name like Bronfman, it's hard not to be known as a Jew, and her mother had converted to the Orthodox stream of Judaism before she was born.

———

At the beginning of my first term as President of the World Jewish Congress, I visited with Rabbi Soloveitchik, the preeminent sage of Jewish life, and asked, "Sir, what advice can you give me, now that I have been elected President of the WJC?" His answer was: "Jews were not put here just to fight anti-Semitism."

I translate that to mean in part that we must do something about the erosion of Judaism—not just in the Diaspora, where it is now very serious, but also in Israel, where many citizens are not only secular, but belligerently so. We must worry more about what we are doing to ourselves rather than always concentrating on what others may be doing to us. To that end, there is an agenda: I firmly believe that we must do two things of fundamental importance: (1) We must endeavor to teach every Jewish child (and in many cases that child's parents) about Judaism, and (2) we must make sure that every Jewish child in the world has a chance to visit Israel.

I have become very involved with Hillel, a group that was founded many years ago by B'nai B'rith to serve Jewish students on campuses. As I visit and talk with the students associated with Jewish campus leadership, they tell me that what motivated them, apart from their Jewish education, was the Israel experience. There are some 400,000 Jews on North American campuses, and this is the last chance we have of keeping them Jewish. With Richard Joel, I have visited many colleges and universities, and will visit many more. I love to talk to the young students, to interface with them, and to challenge them to do what I have learned to do, to study their religion and practice what Richard Joel calls "doing Jewish."

While I am delighted to serve as Chairman of the International Board of Governors, which has become an important part of the Hillel network of financial backing, I am also eager to work with those who want to start teaching high schoolers and their parents about their religion, and then work with those who will teach it to elementary school kids and their parents.

The Samuel Bronfman Foundation, which I chair, started a program some ten years ago, whereby we bring twenty-five high school juniors to Israel for a five-week intensive-study seminar during the summer holiday. The group consists of an even number (if you can split twenty-five evenly) of boys and girls, and also a mixture of all strands of Judaism: Reform, Conservative, Reconstructionist, and Orthodox. The purpose of the program, which is based on merit alone, is to identify and then inspire future Jewish leaders. The director of the program is Rabbi Avi Weinstein, a great scholar and a great educator. While Orthodox, he wins the respect of all his charges, and has instituted a system whereby they stay together as proud "*Bronfmanim*," who constantly use a special e-mail service where they argue and discuss everything from Talmud to date rape. Many of them serve as volunteers to various Jewish organizations once they graduate from college.

At many of the campuses that I visit for Hillel, I run across these bright, challenged, and dedicated students "of mine" and I take enormous pride in their accomplishments.

This program was the successor to a summer camp we started at a place called Afoola. WIZO, the Women's International Zionist Organization, maintained one of their many schools there, and we made use of it for a couple of summers. The camp was for the most part composed of youngsters from mixed marriages who wanted to examine (or whose Jewish parent wanted him or her to examine) Judaism. The third year, we changed to the present program. While I was in Afoola the second summer, some radio reporter shoved a microphone at me and asked a question I didn't understand, except the part that asked if I realized that this, whatever it was, was dividing the Jewish people. Not giving it much thought, I quickly replied that I was against anything that divided the Jewish people.

Back in Jerusalem that evening, I discovered that I was in trouble with the Orthodox organizations that belonged to the WJC. Israel Singer informed me that the issue was about "Who is a Jew?" We interceded with Rabbi Josef Burg, the longtime head of the National Religious Party, and longtime Minister of the Interior, to protest that I never involved myself in matters *Halakha*, Jewish law, and that I was making a political statement about Jewish unity, not a religious one.

He, in turn, got hold of those who were threatening secession and calmed them down.

This was indeed a fractious issue. The reporter's question had been about those people who had been converted by Conservative or Reform rabbis, rather than Orthodox, and whether or not they had the right to the same Law of Return as did the latter. It became a huge issue, and then it died down, but I remember visiting Prime Minister Shamir's office and seeing all sorts of American Jewish leaders line up, waiting to scream and shout over the indignity they all perceived.

In the first place, this whole issue was a molehill turned into a mountain. It affects very few Jews—it basically applies only to intermarriages where the non-Jew converts to Judaism through someone other than an Orthodox rabbi, and makes a difference only if the convert decides to move to Israel. If you add the last qualifier, you are talking about a handful. I believe that with the erosion we see in the Diaspora, it is silly, as well as cruel, to take those who genuinely want to become true partners in marriage, and participate in bringing their children up as Jews, and make life difficult for them. Many in the Reform movement who, when asked what you say to the non-Jewish marriage partner of a Jew, answer, "Welcome." I agree with that position. When my second wife, George, told me she was going to convert, I was not all that enthusiastic, because I believed it was almost impossible to be Jewish if you weren't born into it. But I am very glad she did, because that makes Sara and Clare Jews without any argument—George was converted by an Orthodox rabbi. My own children married outside the faith, but most of my grandchildren are being brought up as Jews.

The buzzword these days has become Jewish Continuity. I dislike that expression; if we continue doing as we have been, we will slide down the slippery slope to a silent and painless Holocaust, the extinction by suicide of Diaspora Jewry. I believe that what we need is a renaissance, a spiritual reawakening that will again make us worthy of being "The Chosen."

The cost of those programs will be quite expensive. I believe that the Jewish tax dollar has to be reexamined, and programs have to be reprioritized. Just as I am entering into discussions with the World Zionist Organization to discuss a merger to save overhead and increase efficiency, so do I believe that the American Jewish community, the most over-organized community known in history, must reexamine its host of organizations on a zero-based budget system. This should be done by the federations who do most of the funding, and monies will be found to make sure that the programs I have advocated, Jewish education and trips to Israel, will be available.

There is still much wrong with this world. Although we

can revel at the end of the Cold War and at the demise of communism, we can also contemplate global warming, the breakdown of the ozone layer, and the terrible problems of overpopulation which threaten to make the planet uninhabitable. The list goes on and on. Do Jews have a role to play in trying to save the environment, in *tikkun olam*, in repairing the world?

When she was eleven, Clare asked me whether it was really worthwhile for her and her generation to work hard at school and prepare themselves for life when the earth was being slowly but surely destroyed.

I said that if people like her cared enough and were vocal enough, it wasn't too late.

Dare we say *"Après moi, le déluge"*? Of course not! As human beings, as Jews, as parents who have brought children into this world, we must fight the battle—all the battles—as long as we draw breath. This is our legacy, and we must pass it on to those who will follow. There has to be a reason the Jews have survived to the last half of the twentieth century to become stronger than ever before. It must be that we have a purpose, and I believe that purpose still is to be "a light unto the nations." Let us get to work, for there is much to be done.